Lambretta
Ll series scooters

SpeedPro Series
- 4-Cylinder Engine – How to Blueprint & Build a Short Block for High Performance by Des Hammill
- Alfa Romeo DOHC High-performance Manual (SpeedPro) by Jim Kartalamakis
- Alfa Romeo Twin Cam Engines – How to Power Tune by Jim Kartalamakis
- Alfa Romeo V6 Engine High-perfomance Manual (SpeedPro) by Jim Kartalamakis
- BMC 998cc A-Series Engine – How to Power Tune by Des Hammill
- The 1275cc A-Series High performance Manual (SpeedPro) by Des Hammill
- Camshafts – How to Choose & Time them for Maximum Power by Des Hammill
- Cylinder Heads – How to Build, Modify & Power Tune Updated & Revised Edition by Peter Burgess
- Distributor-type Ignition Systems – How to Build & Power Tune by Des Hammill
- Fast Road Car – How to Plan and Build New Edition by Daniel Stapleton
- Ford SOHC 'Pinto' & Sierra Cosworth DOHC Engines – How to Power Tune Updated & Enlarged Edition by Des Hammill
- Ford V8 – How to Power Tune Small Block Engines by Des Hammill
- Harley-Davidson Evolution Engines – How to Build & Power Tune by Des Hammill
- Holley Carburetors – How to Build & Power Tune New Edition by Des Hammill
- Jaguar XK Engines – How to Power Tune New Edition by Des Hammill
- MG Midget & Austin-Healey Sprite – How to Power Tune Updated Edition by Daniel Stapleton
- MGB 4-Cylinder Engine – How to Power Tune by Peter Burgess
- MGB V8 Power – Third Edition by Roger Williams
- MGB, MGC & MGB V8 – How to Improve by Roger Williams
- Mini Engines – How to Power Tune on a Small Budget 2nd Edition by Des Hammill
- Motorsport – Getting Started in by SS Collins
- Nitrous Oxide by Trevor Langfield
- Rover V8 Engines – How to Power Tune by Des Hammill
- Sportscar/Kitcar Suspension & Brakes – How to Build & Modify Enlarged & Updated 2nd Edition by Des Hammill
- SU Carburettors – How to Build & Modify for High Performance by Des Hammill
- Suzuki 4WD by John Richardson
- Tiger Avon Sportscar – How to Build Your Own Updated & Revised 2nd Edition by Jim Dudley
- TR2, 3 & TR4 – How to Improve by Roger Williams
- TR5, 250 & TR6 – How to Improve by Roger Williams
- V8 Engine – How to Build a Short Block for High Performance by Des Hammill
- Volkswagen Beetle Suspension, Brakes & Chassis – How to Modify for High Performance by James Hale
- Volkswagen Bus Suspension, Brakes & Chassis – How to Modify for High Performance by James Hale
- Weber DCOE & Dellorto DHLA Carburetors – How to Build & Power Tune 3rd Edition by Des Hammill

Those were the days ... Series
- Alpine Rallies by Martin Pfundner
- Austerity Motoring by Malcolm Bobbitt
- Brighton National Speed Trials by Tony Gardiner
- British Police Cars by Nick Walker
- Crystal Palace by SS Collins
- Dune Buggy Phenomenon by James Hale
- Dune Buggy Phenomenon Volume 2 by James Hale
- Motor Racing at Brands Hatch in the Seventies by Chas Parker
- Motor Racing at Goodwood in the Sixties by Tony Gardiner
- Three Wheelers by Malcolm Bobbitt

Enthusiast's Restoration Manual Series
- Citroën 2CV, How to Restore by Lindsay Porter
- Classic Car Body Work, How to Restore by Martin Thaddeus
- Classic Cars, How to Paint by Martin Thaddeus
- Reliant Regal, How to Restore by Elvis Payne
- Triumph TR2/3/3A, How to Restore by Roger Williams
- Triumph TR4/4A, How to Restore by Roger Williams
- Triumph TR5/250 & 6, How to Restore by Roger Williams
- Triumph TR7/8, How to Restore by Roger Williams
- Volkswagen Beetle, How to Restore by Jim Tyler
- Yamaha FS1-E, How to Restore by John Watts

Essential Buyer's Guide Series
- Alfa GT Buyer's Guide by Keith Booker
- Alfa Romeo Spider by Keith Booker & Jim Talbott
- VW Bus Buyer's Guide by Richard Copping and Ken Cservenka
- Jaguar E-Type Essential Buyer's Guide
- MGB Essential Buyer's Guide
- Porsche 928 Buyer's Guide by David Hemmings
- Triumph TR6 Essential Buyer's Guide
- VW Beetle Buyer's Guide by Ken Cservenka & Richard Copping

Auto-Graphics Series
- Fiat & Abarth by Andrea & David Sparrow
- Jaguar MkII by Andrea & David Sparrow
- Lambretta LI by Andrea & David Sparrow

General
- 1½-litre GP Racing 1961-1965 by MJP Whitelock
- AC Two-litre Saloons & Buckland Sportscars by Leo Archibald
- Alfa Romeo Giulia Coupé GT & GTA by John Tipler
- Alfa Tipo 33 by Ed McDonough & Peter Collins
- American Ford in Miniature by Randall Olson
- Anatomy of the Works Minis by Brian Moylan
- Armstrong-Siddeley by Bill Smith
- Autodrome by SS Collins & Gavin Ireland
- Automotive A-Z, Lane's Dictionary of Automotive Terms by Keith Lane
- Automotive Mascots by David Kay & Lynda Springate
- Bahamas Speed Weeks, The by Terry O'Neil
- Bentley Continental, Corniche and Azure by Martin Bennett
- BMCs Competitions Department Secrets by Stuart Turner, Marcus Chambers & Peter Browning
- BMW 5-Series by Marc Cranswick
- BMW Z-Cars by James Taylor
- British 250cc Racing Motorcycles by Chris Pereira
- British Cars, The Complete Catalogue of, 1895-1975 by David Culshaw & Peter Horrobin
- Bugatti Type 40 by Barrie Price
- Bugatti 46/50 Updated Edition by Barrie Price
- Bugatti 57 2nd Edition by Barrie Price
- Building a Dune Buggy – The Essential Manual by Paul Shakespeare
- Caravans, The Illustrated History 1919-1959 by Andrew Jenkinson
- Caravans, The Illustrated History from 1960 by Andrew Jenkinson
- Chrysler 300 – America's Most Powerful Car 2nd Edition by Robert Ackerson
- Citroën DS by Malcolm Bobbitt
- Cobra – The Real Thing! by Trevor Legate
- Cortina – Ford's Bestseller by Graham Robson
- Coventry Climax Racing Engines by Des Hammill
- Daimler SP250 'Dart' by Brian Long
- Datsun Fairlady Roadster to 280ZX – The Z-car Story by Brian Long
- Ducati 750 Bible, The by Ian Falloon
- Dune Buggy Files by James Hale
- Dune Buggy Handbook by James Hale
- Ferrari Dino – The V6 Ferrari by Brian Long
- Fiat & Abarth 124 Spider & Coupé by John Tipler
- Fiat & Abarth 500 & 600 2nd edition by Malcolm Bobbitt
- Ford F100/F150 Pick-up 1948-1996 by Robert Ackerson
- Ford F150 1997-2005 by Robert Ackerson
- Ford GT40 by Trevor Legate
- Ford Model Y by Sam Roberts
- Ford Thunderbird by Brian Long
- Funky Mopeds by Richard Skelton
- Honda NSX by Brian Long
- Jaguar, The Rise of by Barrie Price
- Jaguar XJ-S by Brian Long
- Jeep CJ by Robert Ackerson
- Jeep Wrangler by Robert Ackerson
- Karmann-Ghia Coupé & Convertible by Malcolm Bobbitt
- Land Rover, The Half-Ton Military by Mark Cook
- Lea-Francis Story, The by Barrie Price
- Lexus Story, The by Brian Long
- Lola – The Illustrated History (1957-1977) by John Starkey
- Lola – All The Sports Racing & Single-Seater Racing Cars 1978-1997 by John Starkey
- Lola T70 – The Racing History & Individual Chassis Record 3rd Edition by John Starkey
- Lotus 49 by Michael Oliver
- Marketingmobiles, The Wonderful Wacky World of by James Hale
- Mazda MX-5/Miata 1.6 Enthusiast's Workshop Manual by Rod Grainger & Pete Shoemark
- Mazda MX-5/Miata 1.8 Enthusiast's Workshop Manual by Rod Grainger & Pete Shoemark
- Mazda MX-5 (& Eunos Roadster) – The World's Favourite Sportscar by Brian Long
- Mazda MX-5 Miata Roadster by Brian Long
- MGA by John Price Williams
- MGB & MGB GT – Expert Guide (Auto-Doc Series) by Roger Williams
- Micro Caravans by Andrew Jenkinson
- Mini Cooper – The Real Thing! by John Tipler
- Mitsubishi Lancer Evo by Brian Long
- Motor Racing Reflections by Anthony Carter
- Motorhomes, The Illustrated History by Andrew Jenkinson
- Motorsport in colour, 1950s by Martyn Wainwright
- MR2 – Toyota's Mid-engined Sports Car by Brian Long
- Nissan 300ZX & 350Z – The Z-car Story by Brian Long
- Pass the Theory and Practical Driving Tests by Clive Gibson & Gavin Hoole
- Pontiac Firebird by Marc Cranswick
- Porsche Boxster by Brian Long
- Porsche 356 by Brian Long
- Porsche 911 Carrera – The Last of the Evolution by Tony Corlett
- Porsche 911, RS & RSR, 4th Edition by John Starkey
- Porsche 911 – The Definitive History 1963-1971 by Brian Long
- Porsche 911 – The Definitive History 1971-1977 by Brian Long
- Porsche 911 – The Definitive History 1977-1987 by Brian Long
- Porsche 911 – The Definitive History 1987-1997 by Brian Long
- Porsche 911 – The Definitive History 1997-2004 by Brian Long
- Porsche 911SC Companion by Adrian Streather
- Porsche 914 The Definitive History Of The Road & Competition Cars by Brian Long
- Porsche 924 by Brian Long
- Porsche 944 by Brian Long
- Porsche 993 'King of Porsche' – The Essential Companion by Adrian Streather
- RAC Rally Action by Tony Gardiner
- Rolls-Royce Silver Shadow/Bentley T Series Corniche & Camargue Revised & Enlarged Edition by Malcolm Bobbitt
- Rolls-Royce Silver Spirit, Silver Spur & Bentley Mulsanne 2nd Edition by Malcolm Bobbitt
- Rolls-Royce Silver Wraith, Dawn & Cloud/Bentley MkVI, R & S Series by Martyn Nutland
- RX-7 – Mazda's Rotary Engine Sportscar (updated & revised new edition) by Brian Long
- Singer Story: Cars, Commercial Vehicles, Bicycles & Motorcycles by Kevin Atkinson
- SM – Citroën's Maserati-engined Supercar by Brian Long
- Subaru Impreza 2nd edition by Brian Long
- Taxi! The Story of the 'London' Taxicab by Malcolm Bobbitt
- Triumph Motorcycles & the Meriden Factory by Hughie Hancox
- Triumph Speed Twin & Thunderbird Bible by Harry Woolridge
- Triumph Tiger Cub Bible by Mike Estall
- Triumph Trophy Bible by Harry Woolridge
- Triumph TR6 by William Kimberley
- Turner's Triumphs, Edward Turner & his Triumph Motorcycles by Jeff Clew
- Velocette Motorcycles - MSS to Thruxton Updated & Revised Edition by Rod Burris
- Volkswagen Bus or Van to Camper, How to Convert by Lindsay Porter
- Volkswagens of the World by Simon Glen
- VW Beetle Cabriolet by Malcolm Bobbitt
- VW Beetle - The Car of the 20th Century by Richard Copping
- VW Bus - 40 years of Splitties, Bays & Wedges by Richard Copping
- VW Bus, Camper, Van, Pickup by Malcolm Bobbitt
- VW Golf by Richard Copping & Ken Cservenka
- VW – The air-cooled era by Richard Copping
- Works Rally Mechanic by Brian Moylan

First published in December 2005 by Veloce Publishing Limited, 33 Trinity Street, Dorchester DT1 1TT England. Fax 01305 268864/e-mail info@veloce.co.uk/web www.veloce.co.uk or www.velocebooks.com
ISBN 13: 978-1-904788-81-2. ISBN 10: 1-904788-81-5. UPC 36847-00381-4 © Andrea & David Sparrow and Veloce Publishing 2005. All rights reserved. With the exception of quoting brief passages for the purpose of review, no part of this publication may be recorded, reproduced or transmitted by any means, including photocopying, without the written permission of Veloce Publishing Ltd. Throughout this book logos, model names and designations, etc, have been used for the purposes of identification, illustration and decoration. Such names are the property of the trademark holder as this is not an official publication.
Readers with ideas for automotive books, or books on other transport or related hobby subjects, are invited to write to the editorial director of Veloce Publishing at the above address. British Library Cataloguing in Publication Data - A catalogue record for this book is available from the British Library.
Printed in the UK by Pims Print.

Lambretta
LI series scooters

Andrea & David Sparrow

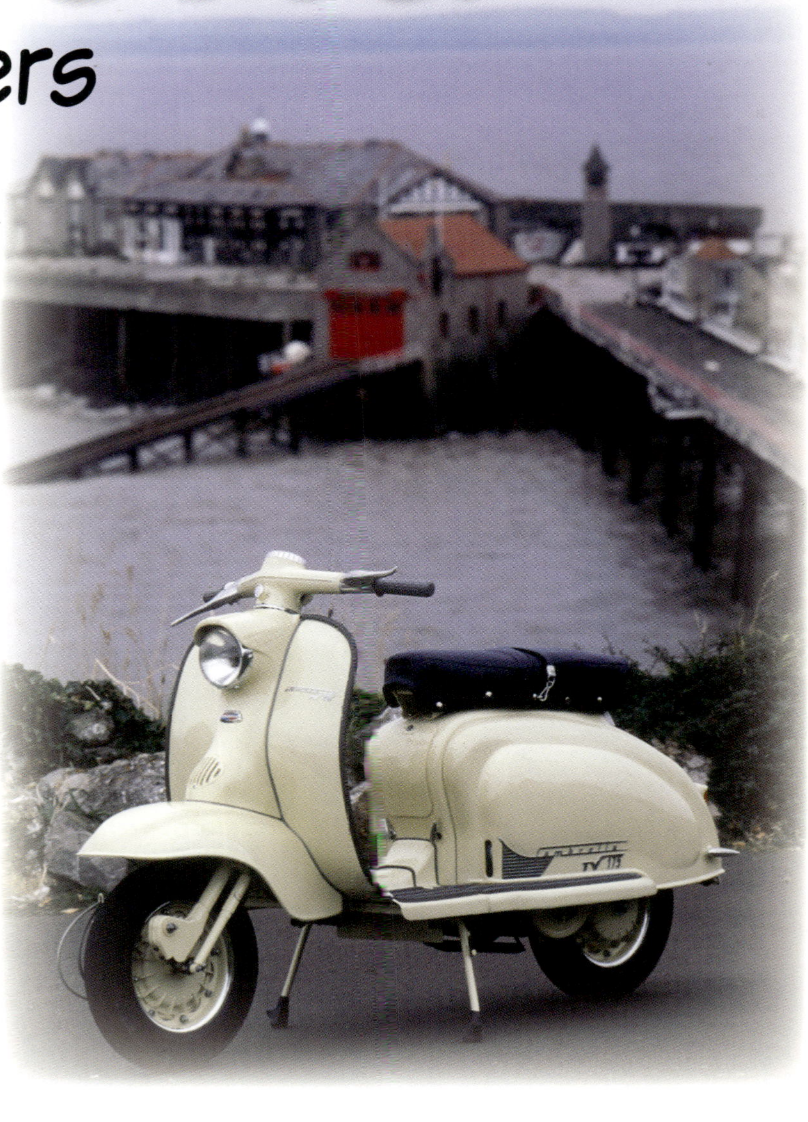

The Lambretta LI Series

Innocenti
The firm that gave the world Lambretta 6

Early days
The first scooters with the name Lambretta 18

In the UK
Lambretta Concessionaires introduces a new scooter 30

Worldwide
Lambretta's fame spreads around the world 42

Variations
Mopeds and Minis, Lambros and the unique little Mink 54

The LI Series
Lambretta's most popular and bestselling model 66

The first Lambrettas had been very successful, although by 1957 the basic style was a decade old. The need for affordable, available transport was as great as ever, but fashion was changing, and the Lambretta would change with it. Following on from the success of the enclosed models, Innocenti introduced a completely new scooter in September 1957. This was the TV 175, the first of the LI Series – the best-loved and most popular Lambretta series of all (LI series 2 model shown).

Innocenti

The firm that gave the world Lambretta

above: Style icons from Milan — a city renowned for cars, bikes, scooters and commercials. Designers and stylists, manufacturers and coachbuilders; many made their home in and around the city. None were more stylish and Milanese than Alfa Romeo and Lambretta.

left: LI150 from 1960, imported into the UK by Lambretta Concessionaires.

A business built on pipes and tubes

Ferdinando Innocenti was born in Brescia, Italy in 1891, and, along with his older brother, joined the family hardware business when he left school. The Innocentis were a technically-minded family with an eye for business – and the company soon branched out into metalwork in general, and steel pipes and tubing in particular.

In 1923 the family moved to Rome with the intention of expanding the hardware business in the new environment of the city. But circumstances conspired against the family – its supporting bank went down, and a winning formula needed to be found. The most likely candidate for success was to expand on the pipe and tube work it was already involved in; there was lots of building going on and such materials were in demand.

So successful was the new venture that a dedicated pipe and tube warehouse opened just three years later. But this entrepreneurial family was not going to rest on its laurels; it started to invent uses, as well as selling the raw materials. First came a sprinkler watering system – and good customers in the shape of the Vatican gardeners. Next came a fire sprinkler system, and new ways of ensuring efficient industrial cooling. Then a quick and easy to assemble scaffolding system – used in the Vatican again, this time for work in the Sistine Chapel. The Vatican provided further work, asking Innocenti to create a tubular frame for a marquee-style hall to house a big Catholic church conference. The company also got involved with that other great Italian passion – football. New stands built in the Rome stadium owed their existence to the Innocenti system.

both pages: TV175 from 1958.

above: LI series II from 1960. The Lambretta's classic lines ensured that it looked good, whether in subtle shades like this cream, or vibrant two-tones like the TV175 from the same year, on the previous page.

right, and page 10: SX200 from 1966. These Lambrettas are now some of the most sought-after by collectors.

above and right: LI150 from 1958. The family resemblance to the enclosed-style Lambretta LC and LD models is clear, but the LI was a new departure, signalling the start of mass market success for the marque.

The benefits of hard work

The Innocentis bucked all the trends. They were in the right place in the right time. They worked extremely hard, both as a company and as individuals. Far from being afraid to try new things, they thought creatively and made inspired choices. As a result, the business was built on a firm footing, increasing its workforce five-fold in just two years.

The business continued to grow. In addition to routine orders for scaffolding and water systems, the company was making electricity pylons and lightning conductors, sprinkler systems and sports equipment, parts for lorries, plant and military vehicles and hydraulic pistons and rollers. It also developed specialized equipment for handling steam and liquid gases.

From 1935, production was largely based in Milan, where the workforce rapidly grew to 200 at the one site alone. This number doubled during the war years, when the factory turned its facilities to the manufacture of aircraft hangars and bomb casings. Work began on a massive new factory of 400,000m^2 in 1939; it was completed in 1942, and provided work for 500 people. However, the building sustained heavy damage in bombing, and would not be fully productive again until 1948.

Luigi Innocenti took over the running of the business on the death of his father in 1966. He carried on the family tradition of hard work and innovation, further strengthening the company.

Ll150 from 1959.

Early days

The first scooters with the name Lambretta

above: Lambretta A model from 1948. Even in the early days there were a number of good colours to choose from.

left: Lambretta C model from 1950. This was the first Lambretta built around a tubular steel frame.

Big business with a social conscience

Of course, Innocenti was not the only company to thrive against the odds. Hard work and determination were the keys to success for any business, and manufacturing operations such as Innocenti had to have a product that people needed, and the service back-up to provide it at the right price and at the right time.

But there was also something special about the Innocenti company; Innocenti senior had envisaged not just success for himself, but the ability to provide work for others. He had set himself the task of providing work at his factory for 6000 people who would otherwise be unemployed – not in order to use them as cheap labour but as a moral choice, with a social objective. Innocenti was blessed with a strong social conscience, and he had brought up his son to feel the same way.

The huge new Innocenti factory in Milan employed thousands of people, and was bursting with facilities. It had a staff canteen that served 5000 meals every day. It had sports and recreational facilities, a swimming pool and a medical centre. It was way ahead of its time. Not surprisingly, people liked to work for Innocenti and, being well-provided for, they gave their best; the company grew strong and successful as a result.

left: Lambretta A model from 1947.

above: Lambretta C model from 1952. The Lambretta's proportions were large enough to take luggage racks and panniers or, as in this case, an additional pillion seat.

above: Lambretta A model from 1948.

right: L1150 with stylish sidecar, from 1959.

The name 'Lambretta' is taken from Lambrate, the name of the site of the state-of-the-art Innocenti factory in the east of Milan.

following pages, left: Lambretta LC model from 1951 – the first model with enclosed bodywork, right: Lambretta LD model from 1958.

The LI's predecessors

The first Lambretta scooter was produced in 1947. Post war, a primary need was to get the economy back on its feet, and cheap, reliable transport was one of the requirements for making this happen. Pondering the usefulness of the lightweight military motorbikes buzzing about in Rome at the time, Innocenti teamed up with Giuseppe Lauro and Pierluigi Torre to create a new form of transport – a motor scooter.

They unveiled their new creation at the Paris Show of 1947. It was already clear from the success of the Vespa – unveiled ahead of its rival – that motor scootering was the way to go. The Lambretta was heralded with a huge marketing and awareness drive, that included radio advertising. An advantage over the Vespa was a more powerful 125cc engine. A commercial version was available from the start.

The first model was officially called 125M but became known as the A model when the B model superseded it in 1948. There was a new tubular frame design for the C model two years later, plus the first enclosed bodywork option, the LC, which, with its leg shields, engine cover panels and rear footplates, was setting the classic scooter shape that would pave the way for future Lambrettas, including the LI. The D and LD models came along in 1951, with an economy E model two years later and the F model the year after that. These were the models that set the standard for Lambretta scooters through the first ten years of production; Luigi Innocenti, meanwhile, was working his way through the ranks (he started as a basic technician), learning his trade in the best way – through hands-on experience with the products.

left: 125FB, based on the B model, from 1949.
right: 150FD, based on the D model, from 1955.

27

Lambretta A model from 1948.

In the UK

Lambretta Concessionaires introduces a new scooter

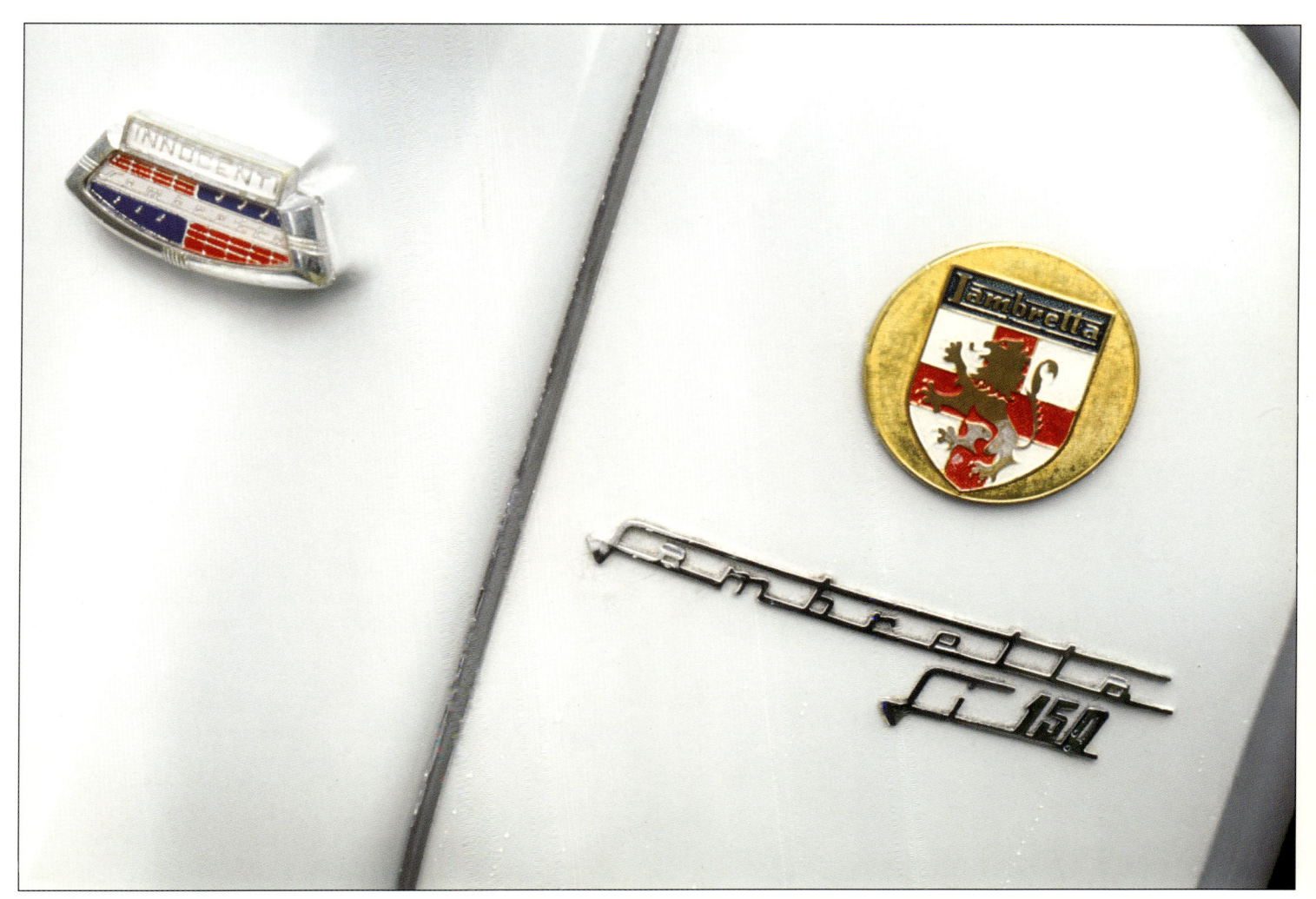

above: An LI150 sporting the badge of UK importer Lambretta Concessionaires.

left: LI150 from 1959.

Lambretta in the UK

As Lambrettas were selling like hot cakes in Italy, it would only be a matter of time before their popularity spread elsewhere. All it took was for the right people to come along. And that's where the Aggs came in. James and Peter Agg's business was founded in 1951 and based in Croydon; they imported C and LC models, and attempted to find motorcycle dealers to take and sell them. This was very hard work at first — the average motorcycle outlet looked down on the scooter as inferior to motorcycles — but gradually things started to change. There were plenty of sales for those who would take the risk, and so the scooter's image improved with success.

Within a couple of years, the Aggs' Lambretta Concessionaires was doing good business. It left nothing to chance: its advertising was ahead of its time; took stands at the Earls Court show; and ensured the Lambretta played every photo opportunity like a star. Each new model was extensively advertised in newspapers and magazines, and editors and journalists were encouraged to ride on, and write about, the latest arrival.

But the Aggs also made sure their advertising was not just a lot of hot air by concentrating on after-sales service too. They set up a chain of 1000 Lambretta service stations, which they required to have every facility to hand for the owner — every part, every accessory, every special approved tool — and they put their mechanics through rigorous company training. Not only did this move impress their customers, it also helped them win new ones, and Lambretta was soon the UK's biggest seller. The Aggs also held the record for most sales of the Lambretta outside Italy — by 1959, 47,000 had been sold, a testament to their skill and determination.

left: SX200 from 1966.
right: TV175 from 1960.

Some Spanish-built machines were imported into the UK by Royspeed, based in Essex. They were high-performance versions and were painted in the Royspeed colours of red, black and gold.

The Rallymaster

In 1961, Lambretta Concessionaires addressed a particular market that was growing in the UK – scooters with a sporting edge. Scooter enthusiasts in the UK were getting passionate about rallies, and a special scooter was needed to tap that market fully. The Rallymaster was designed by Alan Kimber, and based on the Ll150. It was built in the UK and was different to the standard Italian model in a number of ways. Visually it could easily be recognised by the smart black and red horizontal stripes on the engine covers. The front mudguard turned with the steering, it sported a larger rear tyre, a small Perspex windscreen, a spotlight, rally-plate holders and a neat instrument panel boasting a rev counter, a stopwatch holder and an illuminated map holder. It was also fitted with a handle at the rear for assistance in scrambling. The engine was tuned for maximum performance. The Rallymaster remained in production for a little over a year; a smart and distinctive scooter with a devoted sporting following in the UK.

It is clear that the UK scooter market was a little different to the Italian version. The GT200, also known as TV200, made its debut in 1963. It was a particular hit in the UK, as was the Ll150 Special which came out the same year. Both were popular because they were relatively powerful; the gearbox of the Ll150 Special was particularly suited to racing. The Special was known as the Pacemaker in the UK, in homage to the group Gerry and the Pacemakers, which appeared in the scooter's promotions to mutual benefit. A gold Pacemaker sticker, added by Lambretta Concessionaires, provided the finishing touch. Most Pacemakers were silver in colour, but a few were gold, and these were much sought-after.

all pictures: Ll150 Rallymaster from 1961.

37

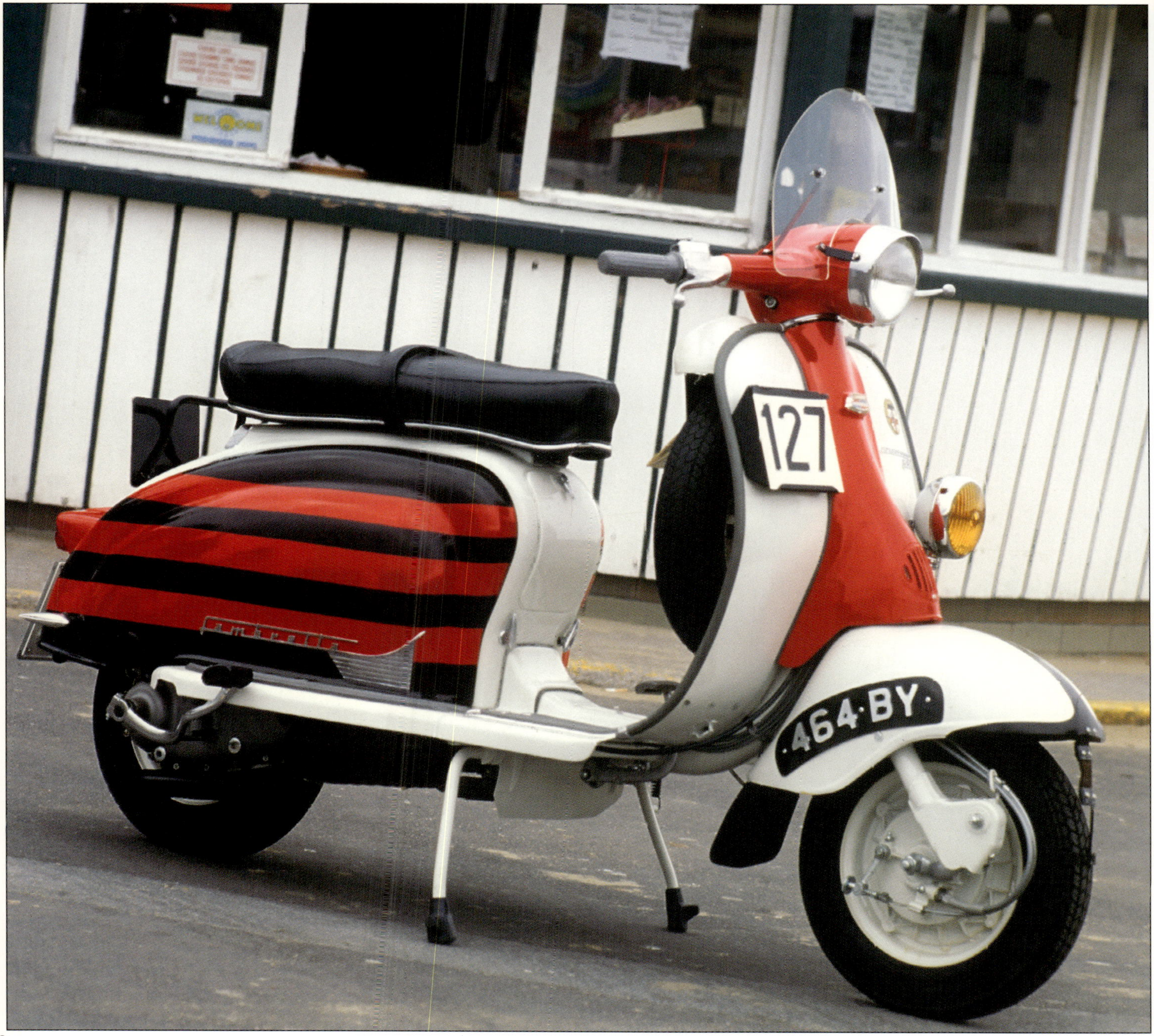
127
464·BY

The Rallymaster's distinctive livery reflected the fact that scootering's image was distinctly sporty in the UK.

In 1960, James and Peter Agg developed a Lambretta scooter with dual controls for training riders in safety. There was a second set of handlebars with controls in front of the pillion seat for the instructor.

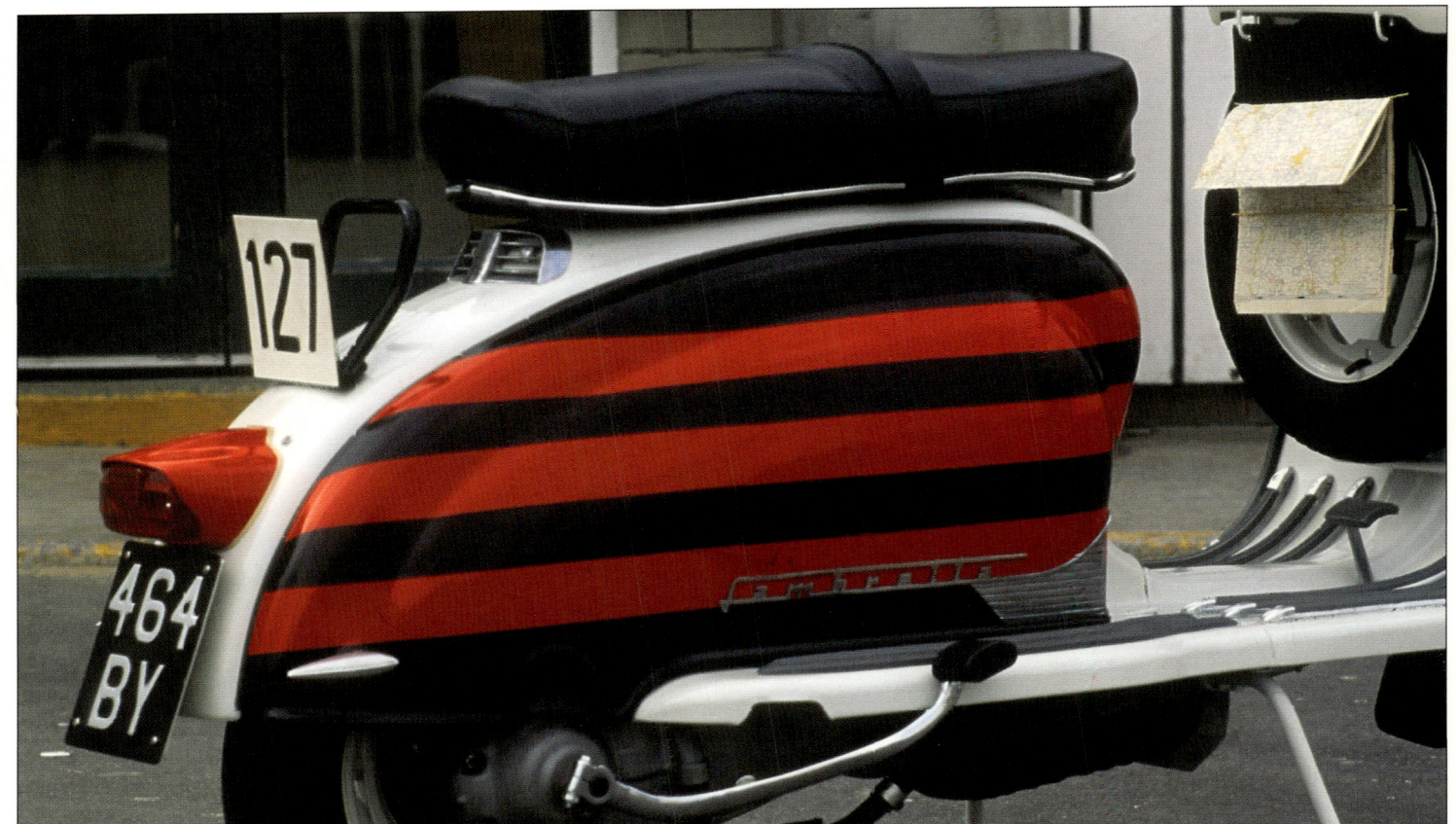

40

Li150 from 1959.

Worldwide

Lambretta's fame spreads around the world

above: 125LD from 1954 made in France by Societe Industrielle de Troyes.

left: The badge of Societe Industrielle de Troyes, the company responsible for Lambrettas in France. The company began manufacture in 1952.

above: A Lambretta made in France under licence from Innocenti.

The fame and popularity of Lambrettas spread throughout Europe. Reliable and cheap to run and maintain, Lambrettas were great for touring, camping and meets with like-minded enthusiasts. There was soon an active and friendly international Lambretta community.

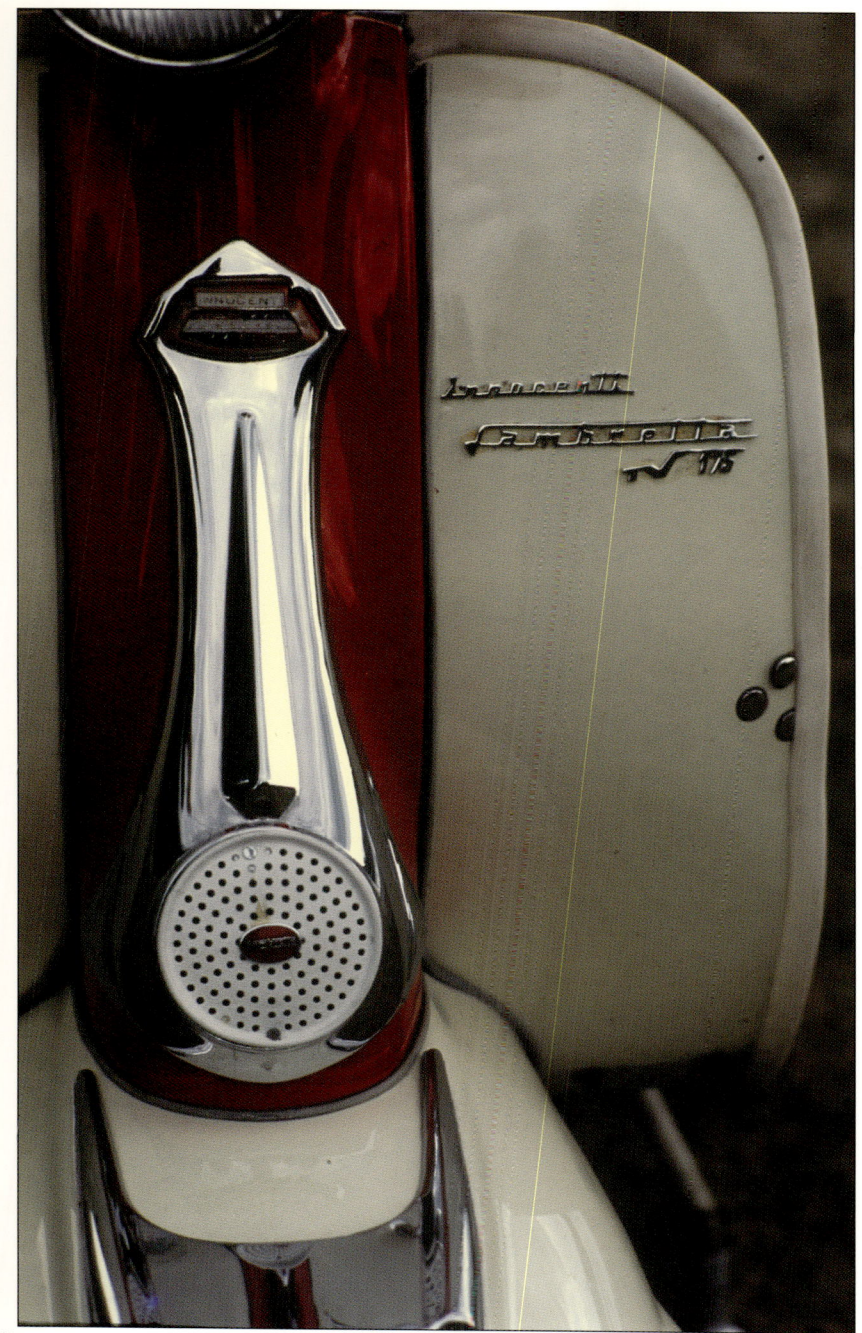

Worldwide Lambretta

Although the spiritual home of the scooter is Italy, it would be wrong to regard scootering as a solely Italian phenomenon. Most of the western European countries, the UK included, had their home-grown scooters as well as importing Vespas and Lambrettas in vast quantities.

In Germany, Lambrettas were manufactured by NSU under license from Innocenti. This arrangement began in 1950, and ended five years later when the German manufacturer brought out a machine of its own design. In France, manufacture of the Lambretta by Societe Industrielle de Troyes started in 1952, and in the same year Lambretta Locomociones SA of Bilbao began to import machines into Spain. Within two years, their popularity was such that the company began manufacturing them under license, and the company name was soon changed to Serveta SA. The LI-based machine it built was called the Lynx, and it also made a 150 Special. Serveta found an export market of its own – they were imported into the USA by Cosmopolitan Motors of Philadelphia for several years.

Outside Europe, Siambretta produced Lambrettas in Argentina which were sold in all South American markets, as were machines imported directly from Italy. In 1955, a deal was struck between Innocenti and Automobile Products of India (API) in Bombay (Mumbai), with the co-operation of the Indian government. Although the Lambretta was slow to sell at first, once it gathered pace there was no stopping it. All the attributes that had endeared it to Italy – low cost, versatility, practicality – made it a winner in India too. The commercial Lambrettas sold particularly well in India. When production of the Lambretta ended in Italy in 1971, the tooling to make the final models was sold to Scooters India Ltd, through the assistance of the Indian government. Innocenti provided technical assistance as part of the deal, and so the Lambretta carried on.

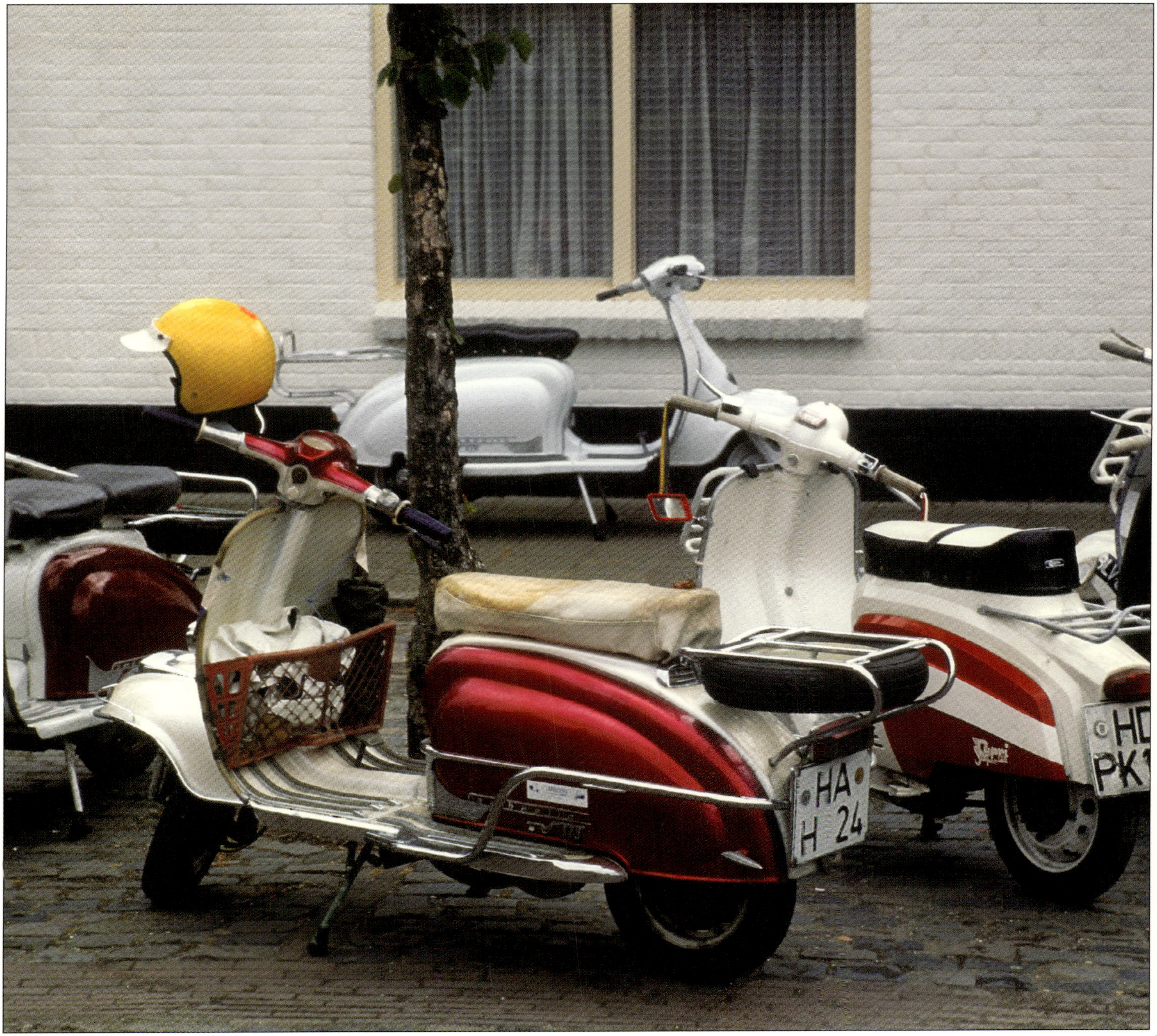
HA
H 24
HD
PK

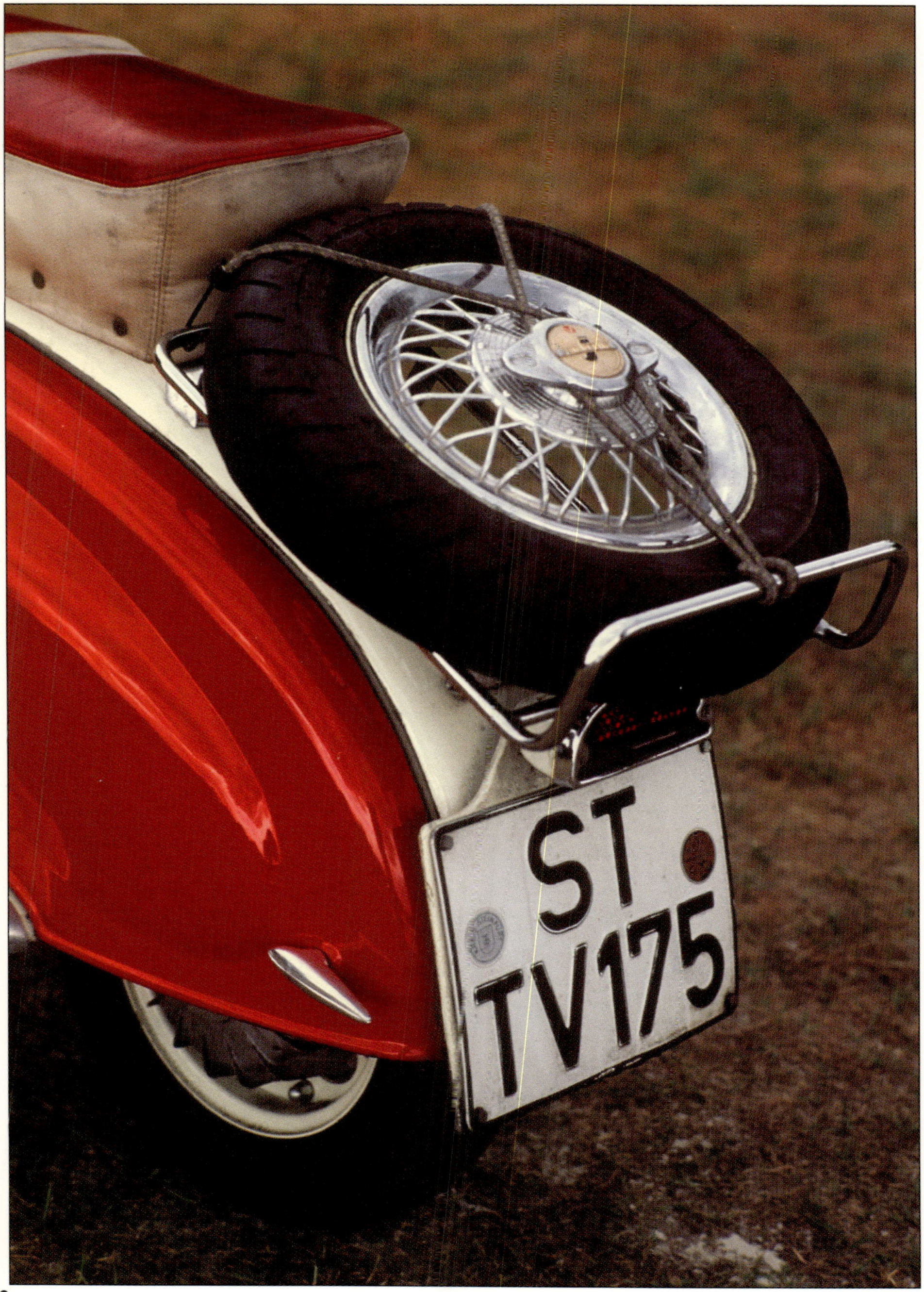
ST
TV175

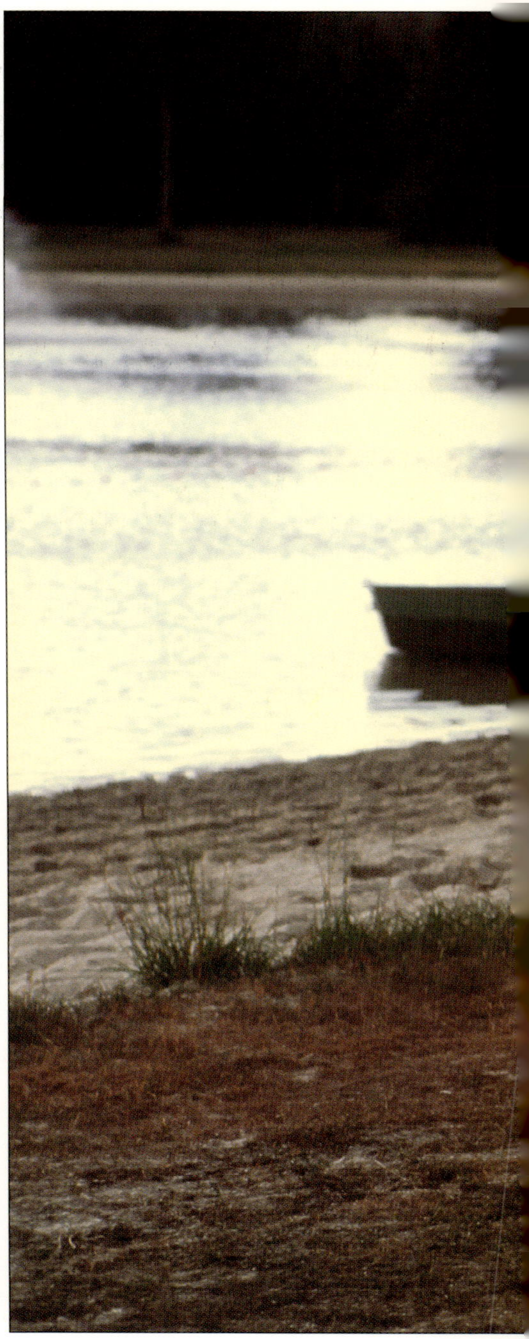

TV175 from 1962 for the German market.

LI125 built by Serveta in Spain. Serveta produced a Lambretta model all its own — the Jet 200 — which continued in production even after Lambretta manufacture in Italy had ended.

Production dates of Lambretta LI Series

LI125	June 1958	Oct 1959
LI150	April 1958	Oct 1959
TV175	Sept 1957	Oct 1959
LI125	Oct 1959	Nov 1961
LI150	Oct 1959	Nov 1961
TV175	Oct 1959	Nov 1961
LI125	Dec 1961	Nov 1967
LI150	Jan 1962	May 1967
TV175	Mar 1962	Oct 1965
TV200	April 1963	Oct 1965
LI150S	Sept 1963	Oct 1966
SX125S	Oct 1965	Jan 1969
SX150	Oct 1966	Jan 1969
SX200	Jan 1966	Jan 1968
GP125	Jan 1969	April 1971
GP150	Jan 1969	April 1971
GP200	Jan 1969	April 1971

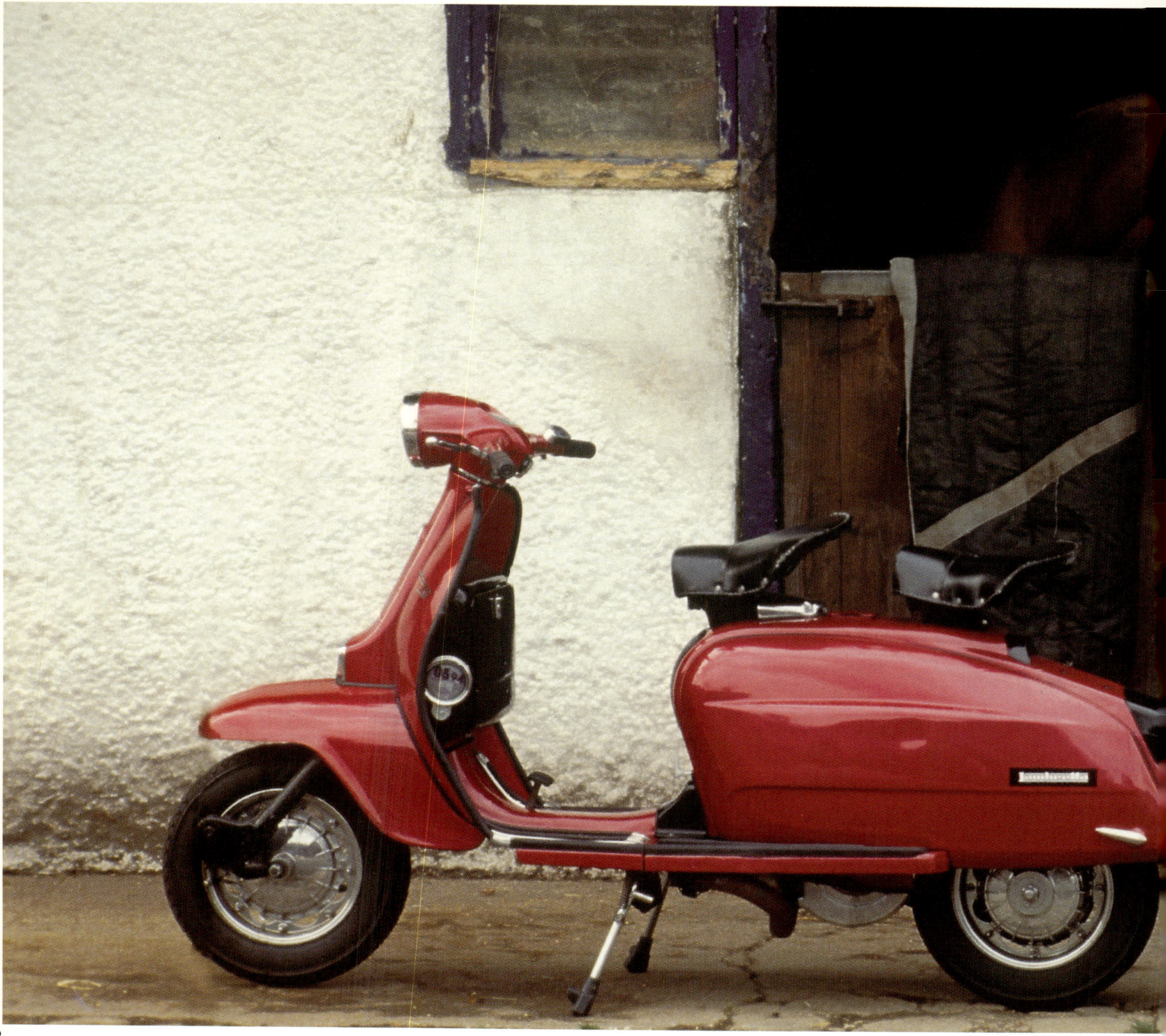

53

Variations

Mopeds and Minis, Lambros and the unique little Mink

55

Scooter to car – the Lambretta Mink

The Mink is literally one of a kind – a prototype small car from the UK that might have been the next big thing in the small world of microcars, had events unknown not conspired against it.

The idea was to create a little car for use in assuredly sunny climates, particularly the island of Bermuda. We do not know why this idea never took root, and why the Mink never made it into production, but the cute little car was destined never to get beyond the prototype stage. Very little is known of its history – only that it was eventually taken out to the country house of a director, to be used by his son for zooming around the grounds. Eventually, when the director retired and sold the house, the Mink came onto the market. It was bought … and sold again, and again, and again, with none of its owners getting around to the restoration task.

Eventually the Mink hit lucky – it was snapped up by microcar enthusiast and expert Mike Webster. Mike restored it to original condition, just as it would have been when first registered in 1968. This was a great deal of work, for chassis, bodywork, brakes and suspension all needed major overhaul. The Mink still runs with its original SX200 engine, with gearing courtesy of a 150cc unit. The mileage of around 4000 miles, Mike believes, is accurate, judging from the condition of the engine, and it has been finished in its original colour. Mike reports that the Mink drives well, with good performance, and is capable of a frightening top speed of 60mph. The two-seater Mink is a little gem – a unique tribute to the adaptability of the Lambretta on which it is based.

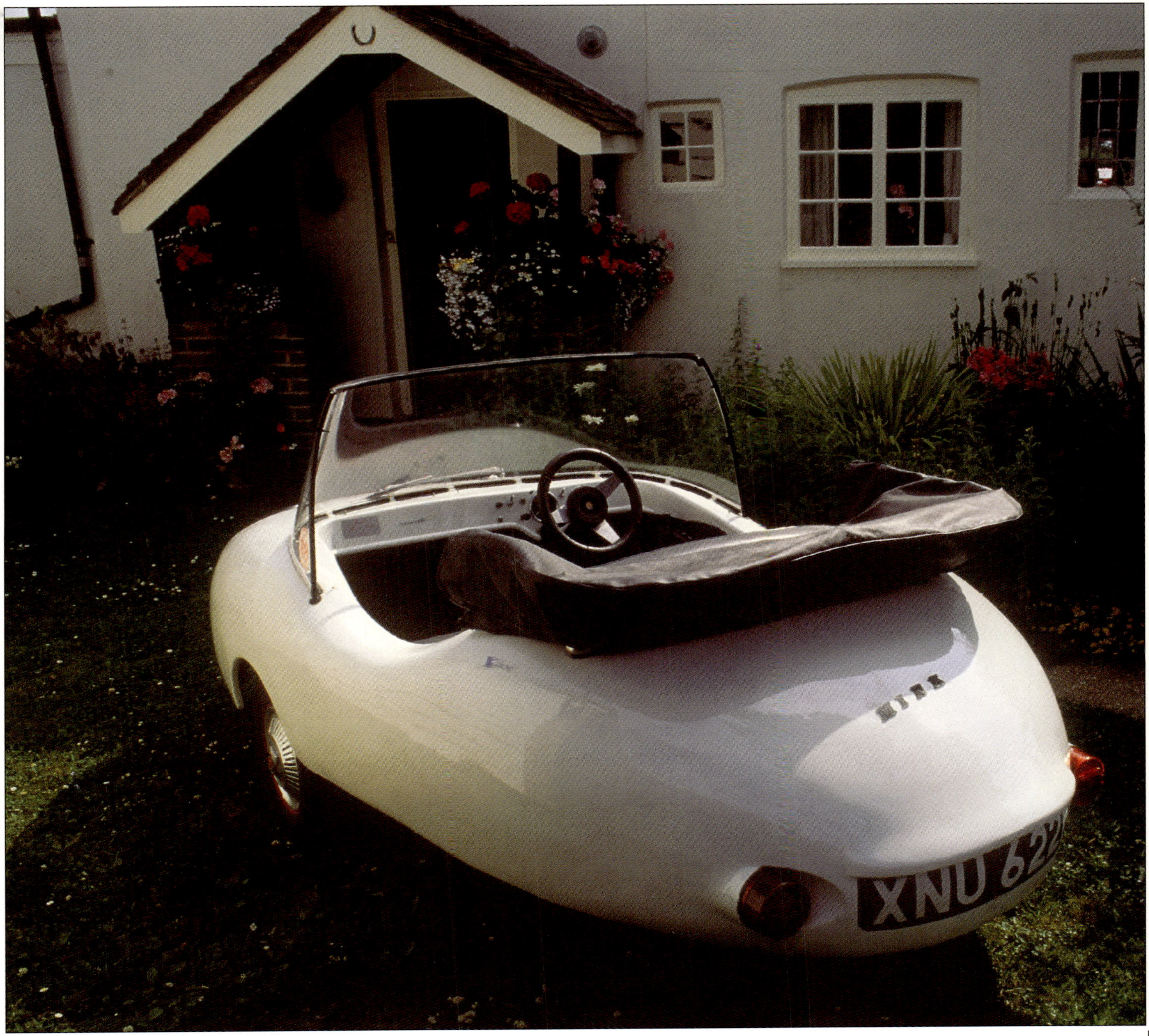
XNU 62

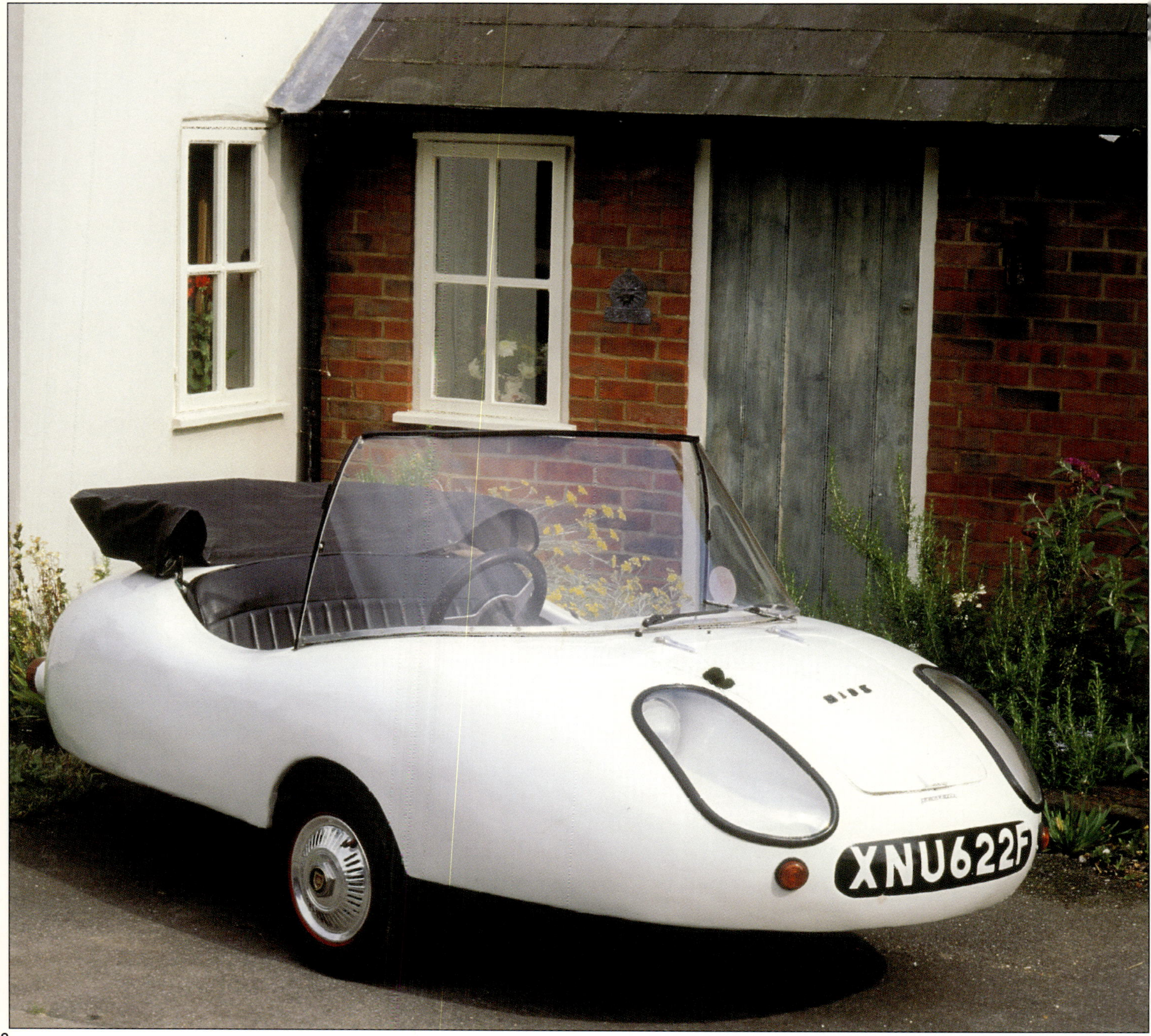
XNU622F

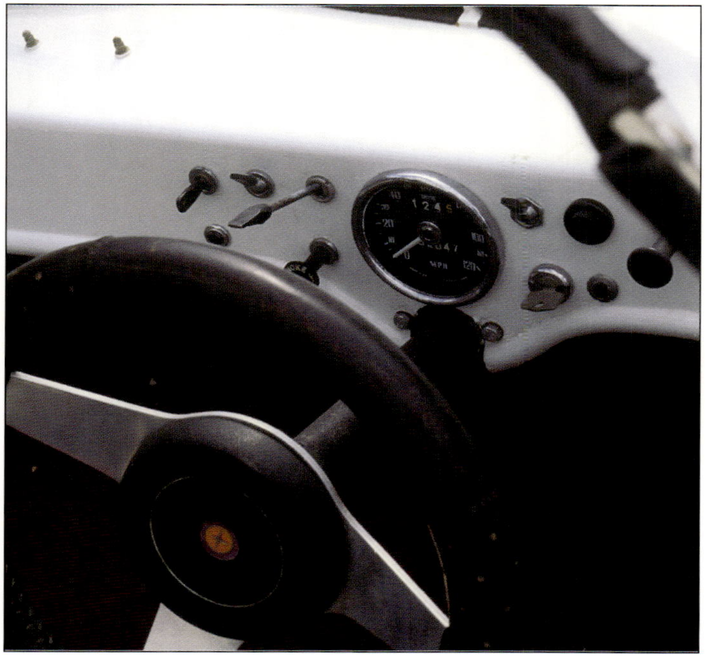

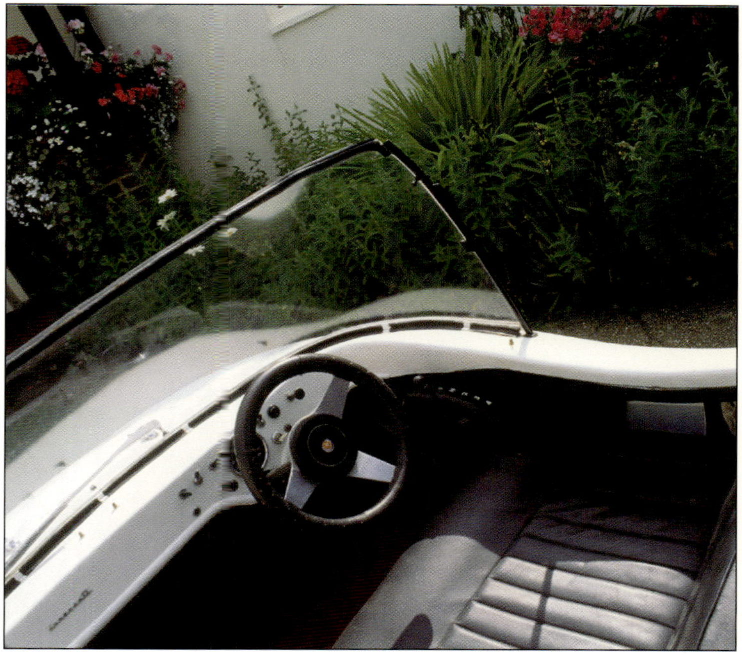

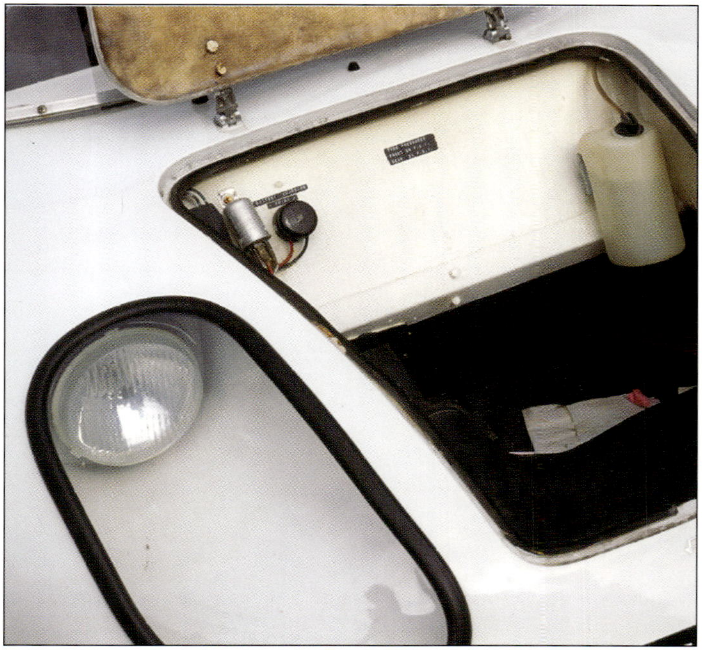

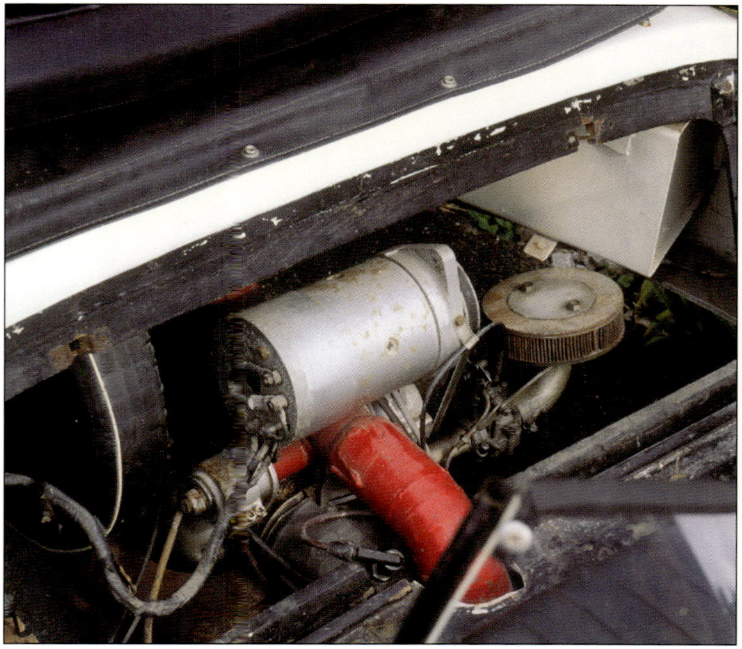

Innocenti's contribution to the motoring world was not confined to the Lambretta scooter. Lambretta also produced two moped models (one of which, the 48 from 1960, is shown below). Scooters and mopeds both had their specific markets; the Lambretta mopeds were popular and well-regarded.

Innocenti brought the famous Mini to Italy. It was expensive, but stylish and desirable, with an aura of sophisticated fun about it. The Mini Cooper badge on the grille of this 1974 Mini was unique to the Innocenti model.

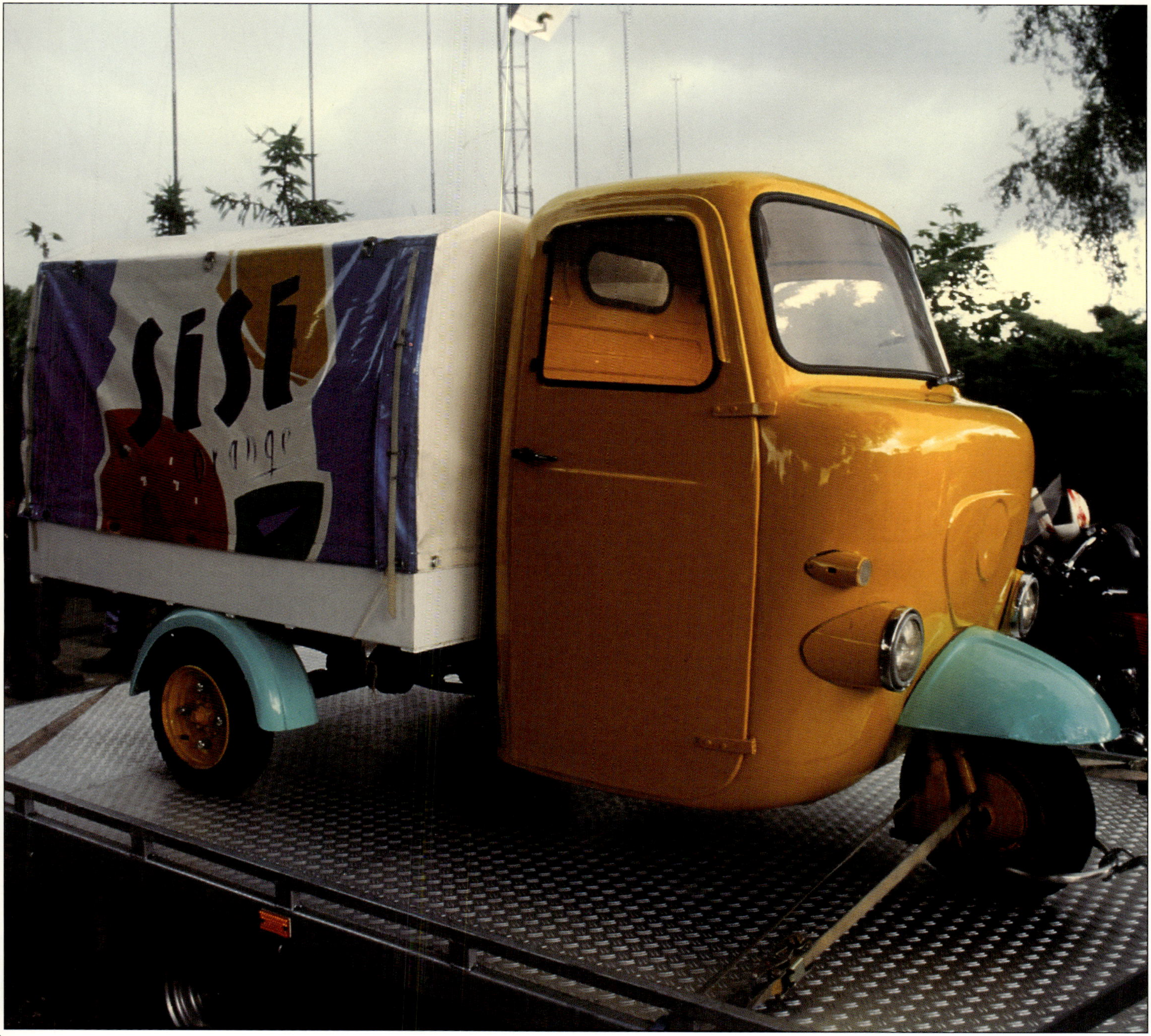
SISI
orange

Commercials – the Lambro Lambrettas

The earliest commercial Lambretta appeared in 1949 alongside the B model. This had the odd formation of a box at the front, and so had one wheel at the rear and two at the front. This made for an interesting drive – if not always a very happy one – but it was a cheap commercial option, and was appreciated for that. Lambros continued to be produced alongside the C and D models, the FDC introduced in October 1957 being the first with an enclosed cab.

The first LI based Lambro was the FLI 175, which made its debut in 1959 as a Series I model. This had a narrow cab, with many of the fittings, including handlebars, coming from the Series I LI. The Series II model replaced it in July 1960, the major change being a wider cab – as wide as the rear box compartment, and a kick start instead of a pull device. Both series were available in several different rear box styles, or alternatively as a chassis only. In this guise it could be used creatively for any number of applications. The Series II was the most popular three-wheeled Lambretta, with more than 70,000 sold during just over five years of production. In June 1963, the Lambro 200, with a larger, 198cc engine joined the range, and continued until 1965.

Summer 1965 brought a new series of Lambros – the 550 and 450, and later 550N – not supersized sporty Lambros with large engines, simply a change in their designation; henceforth the models would be designated by their payloads rather than engine size. Two years later, the engines were moved back behind the cab for the 500L, and the subsequent 550A and V. A further two years on and a new, squarer front shape emerged for the 550M, 500ML and 600M and V; this last was unique in having a car-style steering wheel in place of traditional scooter handlebars.

pictured: Lambro Lambretta 550.

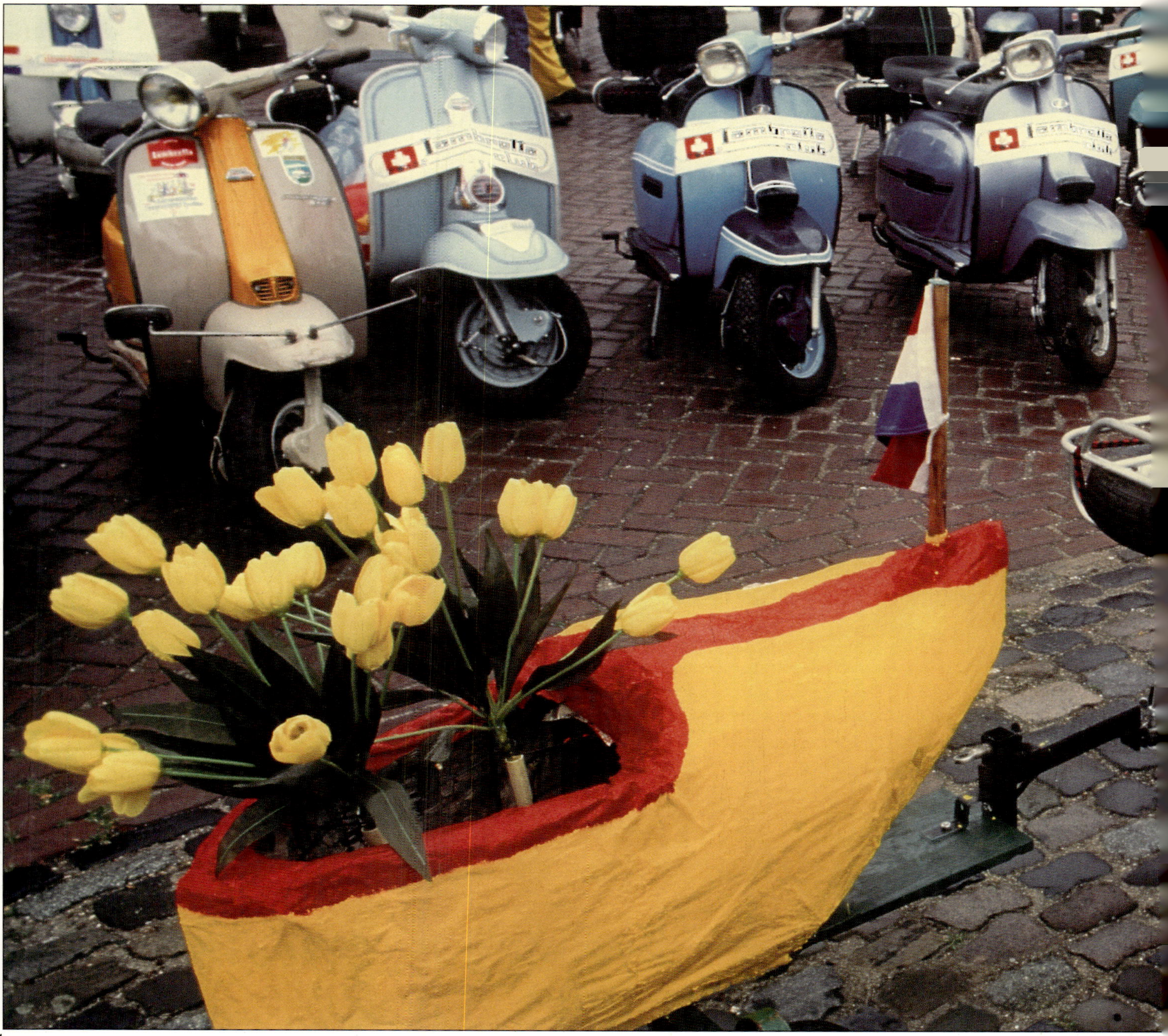
lambretta club
lambretta club
lambretta club

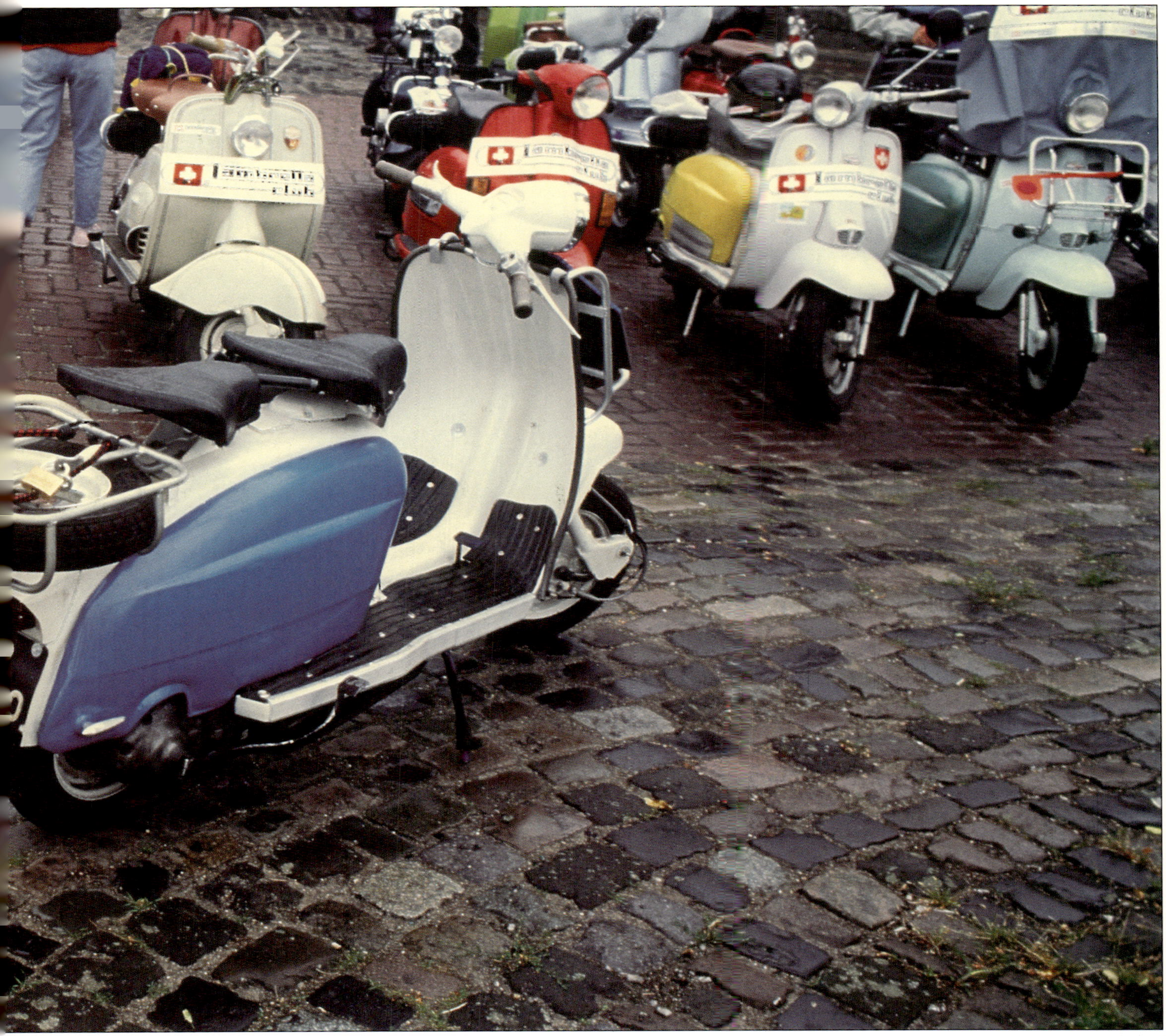

LI Series

Lambretta's most popular and bestselling model

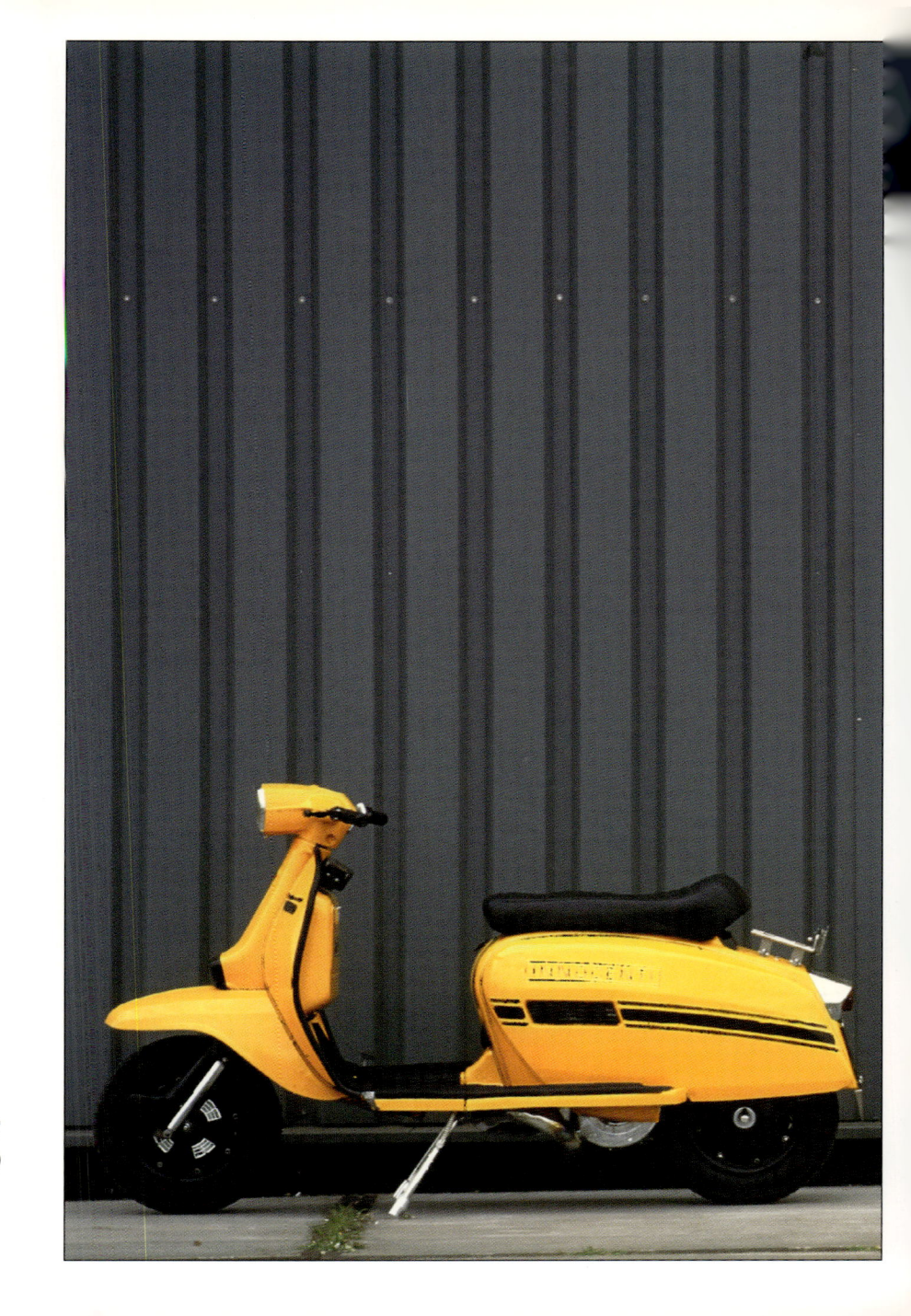

above: TV200 from 1963 – the larger-engined Lambrettas sold particularly well in the UK.

left: GP225 from 1970 (also known as DL for De-Luxe rather than GP for Grand Prix).

67

GP125 (DL125) from 1970 – the GP series was the last of the line. It had modern colours and a sleek shape – but the Lambretta was soon to cease production.

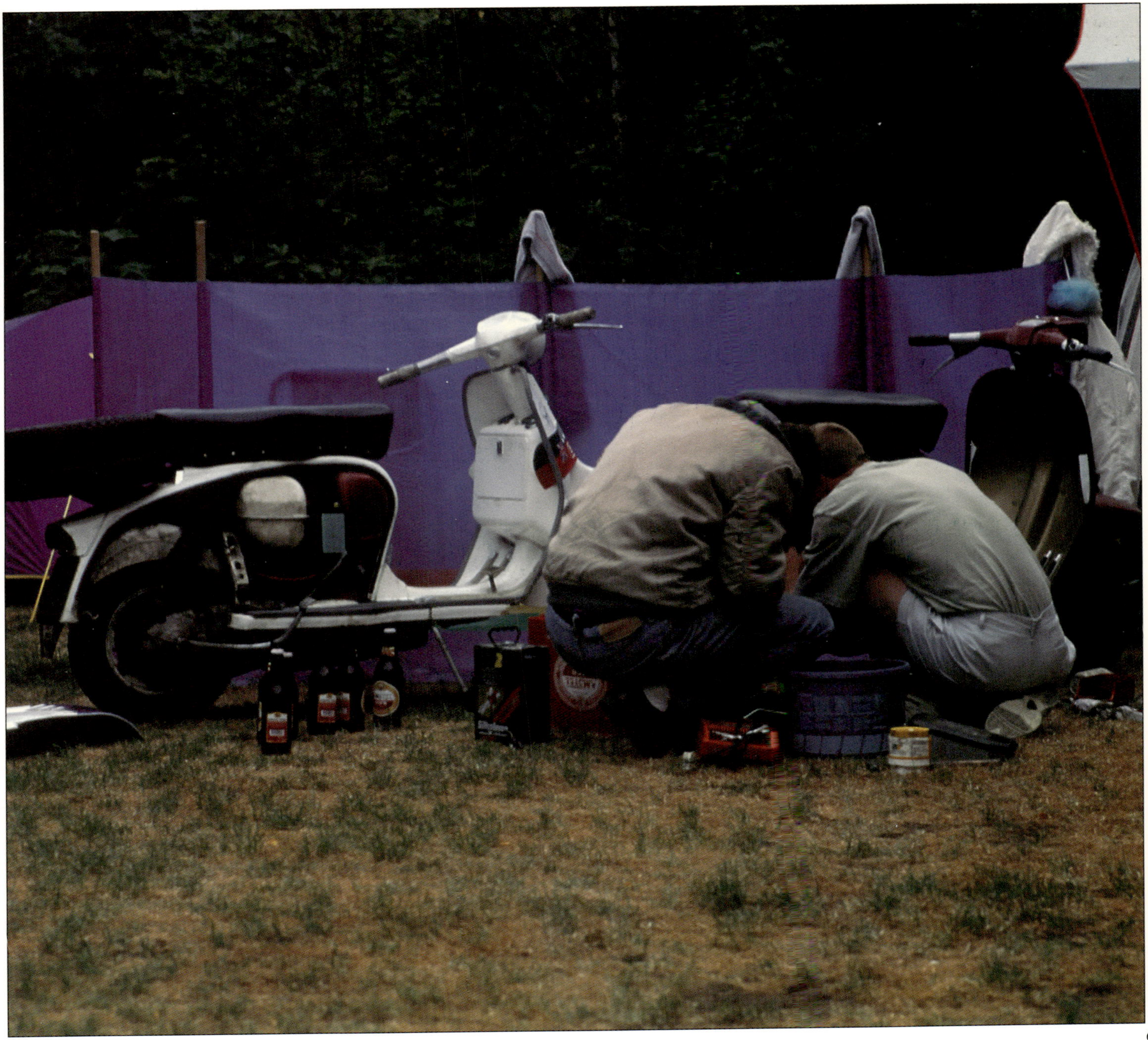

About the LI Series

The first scooter in the new series to make its debut was the TV175, which arrived in September 1957. The LD was still in production – the last of the enclosed, older-style scooters – that would continue in 150LD form until July 1958. The TV was a new concept, an exciting departure from what had gone before. It boasted four gears against its predecessor's three, and the engine was much more powerful, giving a top speed of 64mph. This was a new age of scootering, and Lambretta had risen to the challenge.

The LI itself, in 125 and 150 versions, arrived in spring 1958. The series was completely new, although still based on a tubular steel frame, with a larger front mudguard that did not turn with the steering. The engine was a completely new design. New extras included a speedometer, steering lock, and locking
toolkit under the front seat. This was the Series I LI, which was followed in October 1959 by the Series II. The most obvious change externally was positioning of the headlamp, which moved up to the handlebars. The LI 150 Series II was the most popular Lambretta; it was stable and easy to ride, and came in a range of both bright and pastel colours.

The Series III LI made its debut at Christmas 1961. This LI had a slimmer look, more in keeping with modern 60s styling. The first SX models arrived in October 1965; the SX 200 had specially styled panels for a more sporty look and feel. The last in the LI Series was the GP – also known as the DL. This was styled by Bertone, and featured black rubber trim and bright colour schemes. This is the LI that carries an 'ink spot' on its front mudguard.

pictured: GP225 (DL225) from 1970.

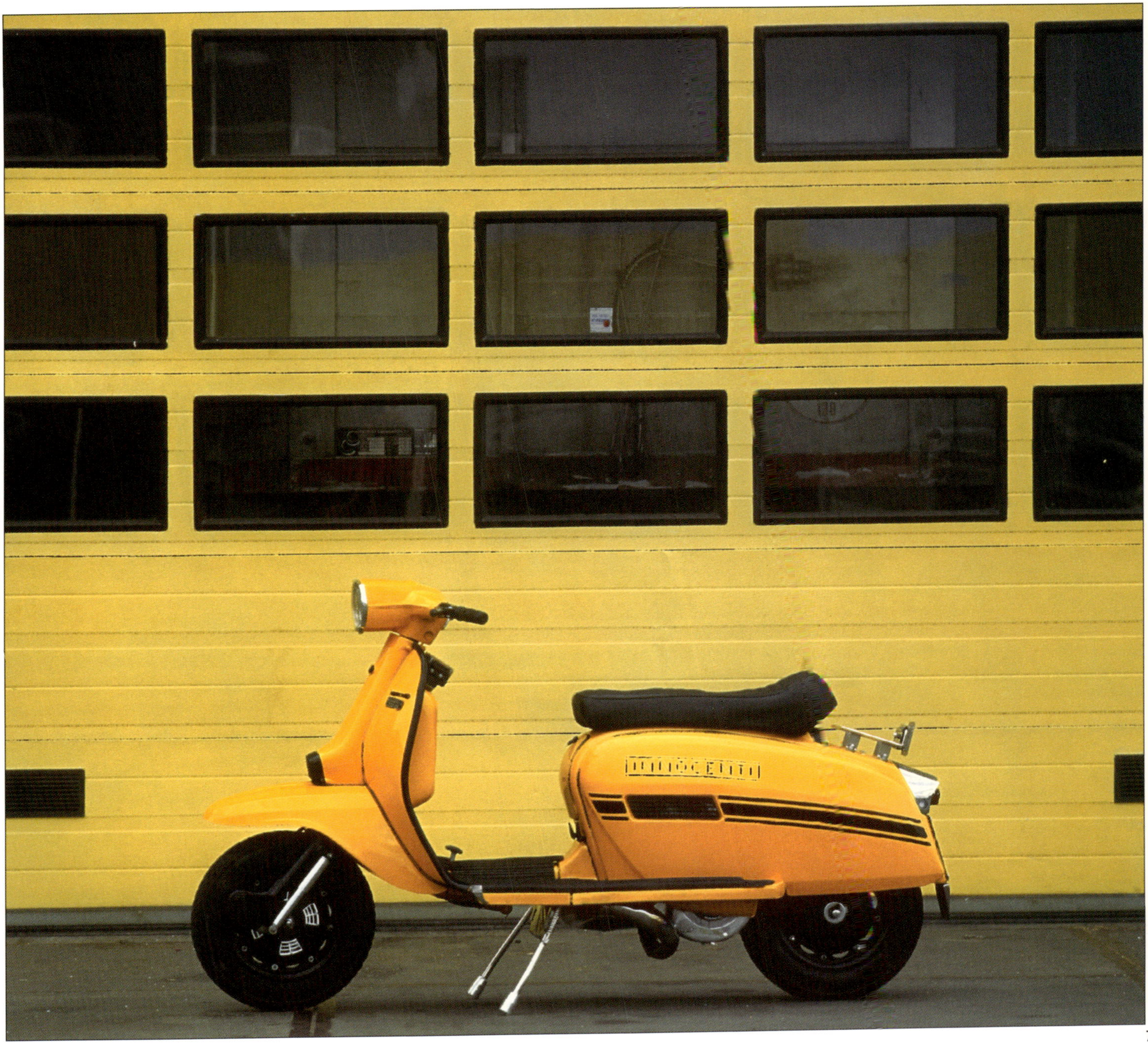

A fantastic L125 with extra accommodation ...

... *a sidecar, ideal for a family trip.*

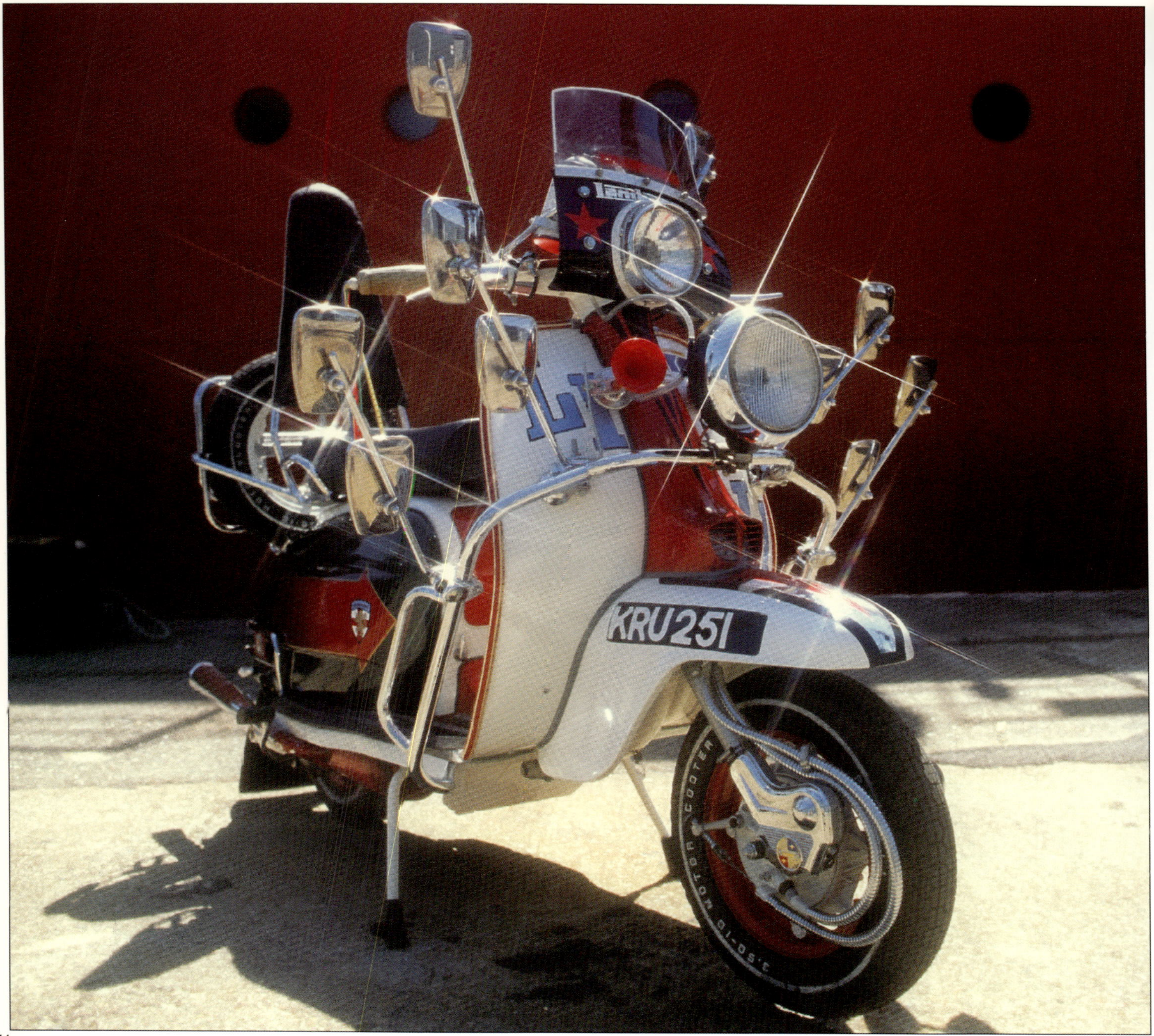
KRU 251

Quadrophenia!

Lambretta aficionado Kev Percival was strolling through Southsea one Sunday afternoon when he first spotted the Lambretta lying on its side at the back of a block of flats. By the time he strolled back the same way later that afternoon, he had resolved to try and find the owner, for he believed that he might be looking at the famous 'Jimmy's scooter' that had starred in the film *Quadrophenia*, released in 1979.

Knocking on a few doors proved fruitless, and Kev was about to give up for the day, when someone appeared from the flats and told him that the scooter's owners had moved away. So it did indeed appear that the scooter had been abandoned, but it also meant that tracing the owners might prove difficult, if not impossible. Kev left a contact number with his informant, and went home, resigned to having reached a dead end. But a few days later the phone rang; it was the scooter's owner, and he was willing to sell it. Kev had meantime made enquiries about the scooter's provenance, and was convinced now that it was the real thing.

And so it was that Kev bought 'Jimmy's scooter.' Kev rebuilt and repainted the LI150, completing it in 1984 and riding it to scooter rallies around the UK. It then hibernated in Kev's garage for almost ten years, re-emerging in the 1990s. Kev spent much time, talent and money restoring it to its film star condition, complete with trademark mirrors, chrome and tassels.

'Jimmy's scooter' – LI150 from 1967.

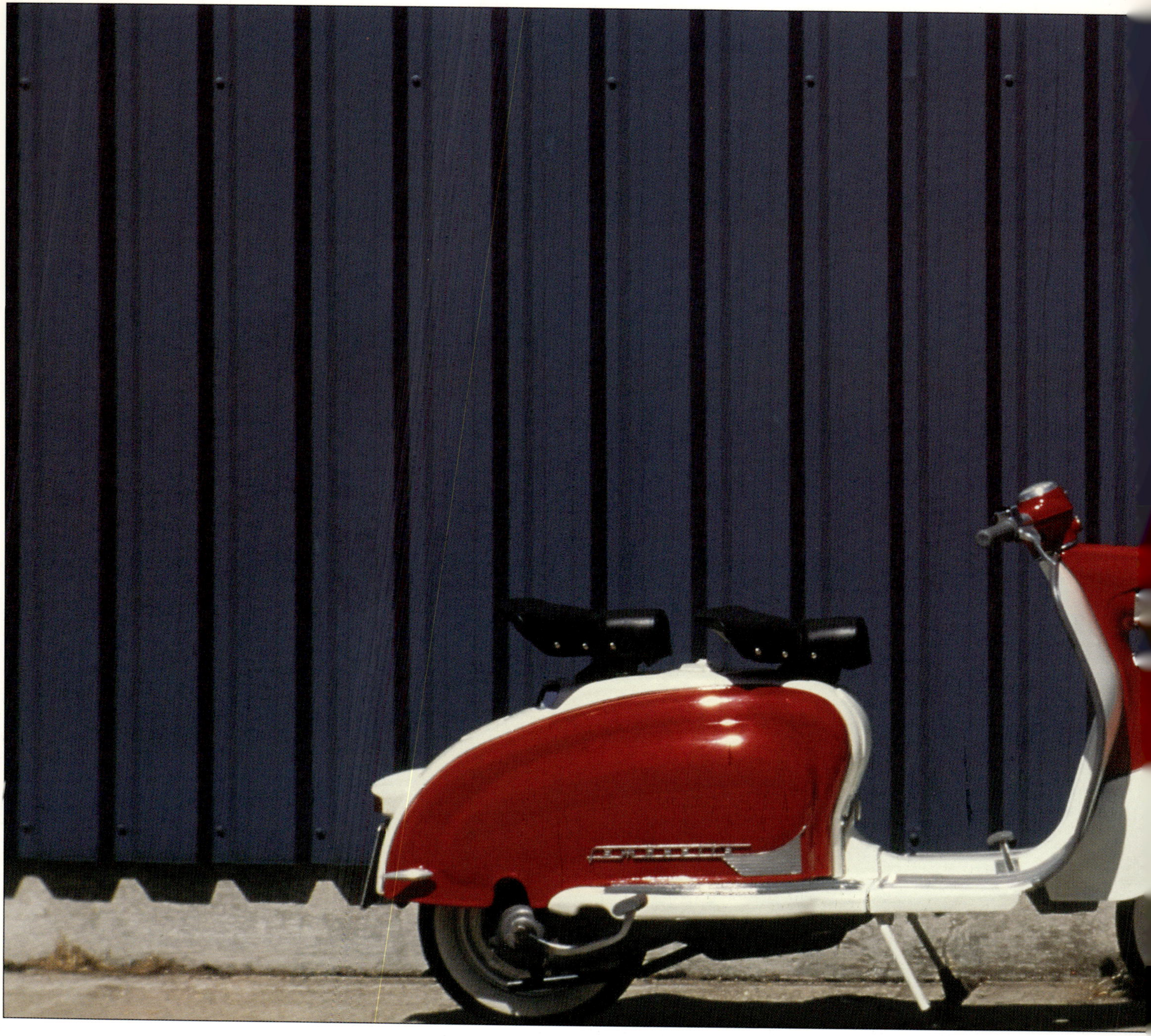

L1150 from 1958.

Thanks

Thank you to all the people that made this book possible – particularly the owners who allowed their scooters to be photographed and shared their memories of experiences with their Lambrettas over the years.

This book is for Roger and Marilyn, with our best wishes.

Index

Agg, James and Peter 32
Alfa Romeo 7
API (Automobile Products India) 46
Argentina 46

Bermuda 56
Bertone 70
Bilbao 46
Bombay (Mumbai) 46
Brescia, Italy 8

Cosmopolitan Motors 46
Croydon, UK 32

Dual controls 39

Earls Court Show, London 32

France 46

Germany 46
Gerry and the Pacemakers 36

India 46
Ink Spot 70
Innocenti Company 5, 8, 15, 20
Innocenti, Ferdinando 8, 20
Innocenti, Luigi 15, 20, 27
Italy 32, 46

Jet 200 50
'Jimmy's scooter' 75

Kimber, Alan 36

Lambrate, Milan 23

Lambretta Concessionaires 32, 36
Lambretta Locomociones SA 46
Lambretta models
    125M (A model) 27
    B model 27
    C model 27, 32
    Commercials 46, 63
    D model 27
    DL 70
    E model 27
    F model 27
    GP 70
    GT200 (TV200) 36
    Jet 200 50
    Lambros 63
    LC model 27, 32
Lambretta models (continued)
    LD model 27, 32, 70
    LI125 70
    LI150 36
    LI150 70
    LI150 Special 36, 46
    Lynx 46
    Pacemaker 36
    Series I, II, III 70
    SX200 70
    TV175 70
    TV200 36
Lambretta name 23
Lauro, Giuseppe 27
Leyland Mini 61

Milan, Italy 7, 15, 20
Mini/Mini Cooper 61
Mink 56

Mopeds 60
Mumbai (Bombay) 46

NSU 46

Paris Show 27
Percival, Kev 75
Philadelphia 46
Production dates 51

Quadrophenia 75

Rallymaster 36
Roman Catholic Church 8
Rome, Italy 8
Royspeed 35

Scooters India Ltd 46
Servetta SA 46, 50
Siambretta 46
Societe Industrielle de Troyes 46
South America 46
Southsea, UK 75
Spain 35

Torre, Pierluigi 27

UK 32, 46
USA 46

Vatican 8
Vespa 27

Webster, Mike 56
World War II 15

Try these other Auto-Graphics series titles from Veloce

Abarth FIAT-based cars
by Andrea & David Sparrow

Packed with 90 superb colour photographs and detailing the full FIAT/Abarth story.

£9.99 ISBN: 1-904788-82-3

Jaguar 'MkI' & MkII saloons
by Andrea & David Sparrow

The story of these quintessentially British cars is complemented by beautiful colour photographs throughout.

£9.99 ISBN: 1-904788-83-1

Visit Veloce on the web - www.velocebooks.com
Special offers • Complete automotive book list • Newsletter • New book news • Gift vouchers